Docudrama Performs the Past

Docudrama Performs the Past:
Arenas of Argument in Films
based on True Stories

By

Steven N. Lipkin

CAMBRIDGE
SCHOLARS
P U B L I S H I N G

Docudrama Performs the Past:
Arenas of Argument in Films based on True Stories,
by Steven N. Lipkin

This book first published 2011

Cambridge Scholars Publishing

12 Back Chapman Street, Newcastle upon Tyne, NE6 2XX, UK

British Library Cataloguing in Publication Data
A catalogue record for this book is available from the British Library

Chapter Seven taken from "*Strange Justice*: Sounding Out the Right: Clarence Thomas, Anita Hill, and Constructing Spin in the Name of Justice." *Jump Cut* 48:2006: http://www.ejumpcut.org/archive/jc48.2006/ClarThomas/index.html

Chapter Eight taken from *Ethics and Entertainment: Essays on Media Culture and Media Morality* © 2010. Edited by Howard Good and Sandra L. Borden. By kind permission of McFarland & Company Inc., Box 611, Jefferson NC 28640 (www.mcfarlandpub.com).

Chapter Eleven taken from "'Movie-of-the-Week' Docudrama, 'Historical Event' Television and Steven Spielberg's Series *Band of Brothers*". *New Review of Film and Television Studies* 7:1 93-107 © 2001. Edited by Derek Paget and Steven N. Lipkin. By kind permission of Taylor and Francis Group (http://www.informaworld.com).

Chapter Twelve taken from *The Relatable Real: Docudrama, Ethics, and Saving Jessica Lynch.* © *Jump Cut* ("The Relatable Real: Docudrama, Ethics, and *Saving Jessica Lynch*." *Jump Cut* 47:2005: http://www.ejumpcut.org/archive/jc47.2005/lipkin/index.html_)

ISBN (10): 1-4438-2682-0, ISBN (13): 978-1-4438-2682-2

For My Family

TABLE OF CONTENTS

ACKNOWLEDGEMENTS

Docudrama Performs the Past begins where *Real Emotional Logic* ended, with the new millennium's remarkable persistence of productions of feature films and movies-of-the-week "based on true stories." While this book, much in the vein of its predecessor, strives to explore the facets of the cinematic persuasion that producers and audiences, for various reasons, find so useful, it does so by embracing the recognition that docudramatic re-creation performs people and events of the past, and consequently its performance contributes importantly, and at its best responsibly, to public memory.

The focus here on docudrama's interplay between performance and memory has benefited from a number of influences. Derek Paget has brought "Acting With Facts" in film, theatre, and television to the foreground of scholarship in these disciplines through his leadership of the Arts and Humanities Research Council of England grant project by that same name, as well as through many fruitful years of advice, collaboration, and friendship. I also must thank Nancy Lipkin Stein for invaluable guidance through the connections between the fields of rhetoric and public memory studies. Alan Rosenthal, in generously sharing his wisdom of the necessary balance between theory and practice, has repeatedly helped return my thinking to the ethical dimensions of the ways docudrama shapes public memory.

Among the many who have helped through their interest in this effort, I owe great thanks to: Martyn Burke, Rowdy Herrington, and David Alan Basche for generously sharing their time and perceptions of their work; Kevin Hagopian for years of insight and true collegiality; Peter Hughes, Jane Roscoe, Debra Beattie, Tobbias Ebbrecht, Richard Kilborn, Julia Lesage, John Parris Springer, and Sandy Borden for sage advice; the entire Acting With Facts group for their interest and support; and my colleagues and students at Western Michigan University.

CHAPTER ONE

ARENAS OF RE-CREATION: EVENTS DOCUDRAMA, WAR DOCUDRAMA, AND THE BIOPIC

> "We actually shot in the house where Mary Malone grew up. In the scene where she's talking to Bobby [Jones] on the telephone? And her father's sitting there? That's Mary's house. I said, this is the stairway she really went up, this is where her father was sitting, this is all real. I think everybody got lit up by it pretty well."
> —Rowdy Herrington, Writer/Director, *Bobby Jones: Stroke of Genius*[1]

Understanding how docudrama performs the past rests upon three basic presuppositions:

First, as docudramas re-create actual people and events these works perform their material. Simply put, docudramatic re-creation is performance. Docudramas, films and movies-of-the-week based on true stories, hinge their appeal on re-creating actual people and events. The premises of the persuasive arguments docudramas forward accordingly work within the basic settings allowed by noteworthy events, and the lives of noteworthy individuals. Docudramatic performance appears to us within these settings.

Second, as docudramas perform the past, they offer us a performance of memory. Through these performances the memories of others become ours. The performance of memory warrants—grounds—docudramatic representation in actuality, and indicates the sense of obligation to the past that helps make docudrama a distinctive mode of representation.

Third, the spirit of obligation to the past frames the ethical considerations docudrama raises, as performance in docudrama shapes public memory.

These suggestions have ties to ideas I've developed previously in *Real Emotional Logic: Film and Television Docudrama as Persuasive Practice.*[2]

In that book I forwarded the view that docudrama is a mode of presentation made distinct by what warrants its representations of its material. To clarify, docudrama works as a mode of presentation, rather than as a film genre. Docudrama is not a kind or type of story, but rather a means of representation, a way of offering argument about the past. The work of re-creating actual people and events suggests that it makes more sense to view docudrama as a mode of storytelling, rather than a singular story genre. Docudrama's reasoning from setting becomes a fundamental characteristic of how docudrama operates as a mode of representation.

While substantial scholarly energy has been devoted to film genre theory[3] the idea of "modes" in film has not received much attention. In his *American Cinema/American Culture*, for example, John Belton refers to melodrama as one of several "modal genres" without further explanation of what this means.[4] Belton is suggesting that melodramas, like musicals, become identifiable through foregrounded formal elements, their means of presentation. In *Representing Reality* documentary film scholar Bill Nichols distinguishes between several modes of documentary film, including the poetic, expository, observational, participatory, reflexive, and performative modes, characterized and differentiated by how the technology of representation mediates the relationships between subject, audience, and filmmaker.[5]   Both Belton and Nichols work with modes of filmic representation by emphasizing not what is represented, a focus more in the spirit of genre theory, but rather how representation works.

I've suggested that docudrama works as a mode of presentation in its fusion of documentary material (its "actual" subject matter), and the structures and strategies of classic Hollywood narrative form, including character development, conflict, and closure.[6] Performance also distinguishes docudrama as a mode, since docudrama foregrounds what it represents as performance, however it is a performance of the actual.   To see this, consider how foregrounding performance creates a kinship bond between docudrama and reality TV. John Corner, for example, in examining the same kind of foregrounding in reality TV has referred to the work of framing, staging, and narrating simulated documentary material as "performing the real."[7] This differs from docudrama, however, since there is no actual memory to perform. To paraphrase Bill Nichols, reality TV becomes distinct as it gives us one performance too many.[8] But the two modes share the work of foregrounding performance. Markers such as star casting, and feature film advertising, distribution, and exhibition remind us emphatically that docudrama performs what it re-creates. What is important here, however, is that docudramatic re-creation warrants its representation by performing a memory of the past.

I have proposed that docudrama's persuasive logic depends upon warrants.[9] Warrants ground docudramatic representation in the actuality it represents. Warrants in docudrama include models (indexically iconic representations, or motivated resemblances to their actual referents), sequences (alternating images of actual and re-created material), and interactions of real and re-created materials within the same screen space. Warrants link and authenticate the evidence and the claims that docudramas forward. The performance of memory in docudrama also warrants claims about the past. Representing memory grounds the representation in actuality, authenticating and legitimating the argument, the view of the past, that we are watching. A film such as *Flags of Our Fathers* (C. Eastwood, 2006) further shows that docudrama can perform various kinds of memory, however when docudrama performs the past its representations most importantly become part of public memory, pressing historical and ethical obligations upon all facets of the work of performing the past. I will view "memory" here as the performance of the past, a view that distinguishes between memory as a process (and consequently the subject of cognitive theory and methodologies), and the filmic representation of that process and what is remembered ("memories").

Docudrama's performance of the past—its performance of memory and memories—falls into several further modes of docudramatic argument that I suggest we envision as "arenas" of presentation. Arenas of the performance of memory keep our attention drawn to the space within which we see roles fulfilled. Arenas of action, like those within which sporting events occur, are ritualistic spaces, coded by norms, rules, and expectations. As realms of representation arenas balance equally the import and functions of action, setting, and text. Within the arenas that docudramas perform memory occurs the reciprocal legibility of setting and action: in brief, we read the one through, and because of, the other.

Docudrama's fundamental work of shaping our memory of actual people and events through its work of re-creation creates three broad and flexible kinds of settings, the arenas of docudramatic representation. The arenas that frame docudrama's performance of memory accordingly include the representation of noteworthy events (*United 93*; *The Perfect Storm*; *Frost/Nixon*); the representation of the events of war (such as *Defiance* and *Flags Of Our Fathers* serve to illustrate); and the representation of noteworthy individuals in the biopic. Looking at specific works suggests that arenas can provide staging grounds separately or in unison. As modes of representation they are ways or manners of operating, and so the issue is not accomplishing strict categorization, but seeing, for example, how what characterizes the means of representation in an events docudrama and in the biopic might work in unison in films such as *Charlie Wilson's War*, *The Insider*, or *The Greatest Game Ever Played*.

One result of viewing docudrama as working within arenas of the performance of memory is that it mandates attention to setting. It allows us to ask, what relates acting to context, to the literal and figurative stages that frame it? While there has been a great deal of valuable work recently on screen acting, this research has been largely focused on technique. The material in Cindy Baron's and Sharon Carnicke's *Reframing Screen Performance* and most of the essays anthologized in the earlier *More Than A Method*, edited by Cindy Baron, Diane Carson, and Frank P. Tomasulo, understandably focus on describing "screen acting," how it can be related to Stanislavskian training, and generally return to matters of technique, gesture, and expression.[10] Baron and Carnicke in *Reframing* situate acting within film's larger formal system and the case studies that follow consider the impact of lighting, editing, shot framing, and sound on film performance.[11] Frank P. Tomasulo's "The Sounds of Silence: Modernist Acting in Michelangelo Antonioni's *Blow-up*" in *More Than a Method* relates actors and the film's acting to the filmed environment, noting: "Indeed, the Antonioni character is often just a small part of a larger visual and social field ... By foregrounding the background, Antonioni redefines the nature of film dramaturgy—and the nature of cinematic performance."[12] Tomasulo is suggesting a useful distinction between acting, and the craft elements inherent to acting for film, and performance, which we can understand to be role behavior (purposeful action) within physical space and cultural contexts. Diane Carson's essay in *More than A Method* on John Sayles's *Matewan* (1987), also in the anthology's section on modernist acting theory, considers how location helps feed the authenticity of performance, which comes much closer to what I see happening in docudramas that often re-create events that have happened in the places where they occurred or close to it.[13] Within recent literature on screen acting then there is at least some indication that we should consider the reciprocality between action on screen and the space within which it occurs.

The arenas that frame performance become the means to make the past present. Arenas create the staging ground for contestation, confrontation, and engagement. Identity and action intersect within the arena. It is precisely because of the arena that who one is, where one is, and what one does become reciprocally legible. Through place—the space of the arena—action and identity define each other. The arena produces action. Character action becomes a consequence of the codes that give the arena its shape, structure, and form. The arena fits within a larger social system and is recognizable as a staging ground because of the structures, rules, and processes that characterize it. As it fits within a larger social system the arena expresses and reinforces social codes. Sports provide us with a multitude of examples of arenas. The ropes and canvas that frame a boxing ring provide the physical space that activates the rules and strategies of boxers, actors whose identities are defined by the actions performed within the space of the ring. One could say the same of a baseball diamond, a cricket pitch, or a football field.

The "arenas" that ground action within place in docudramas about noteworthy events, people, and war provide memorable forms to frame action and identity. We see what happens within the arena as both relatable and moral. Since the actions that occur within arenas have the purpose of attaining goals what we see within these arenas becomes relatable. We might not share a goal but we can relate to—understand and identify with—the necessary effort that has to be expended to attain it. The variety of emotional, cognitive, and optical point of view structures we find in the performance of the past also ensure that we relate to what the arena enacts for us.[14] Arenas create a space of contestation that presupposes a moral system. The arena allows us to view the processes of winning and losing in a moral light. The arena addresses the questions, is it right or wrong to win or lose? Any goal attained within the arena becomes illuminated by the moral light inherent to how the arena functions.

The notion of "arenas" of representation is also appropriate to the multifaceted nature of memory—the idea that remembering something that's happened presupposes not only action (what we did, or what was done to us) but also where (and how) such action occurred. Consequently when docudrama performs the past it becomes public memory through the functions of these arenas of performance. Noteworthy events and events in war become selected, arranged, and morally framed as they enter the realm of public memory through arenas of docudramatic presentation. In the case of the biopic, personal memory similarly becomes public property. In assessing the effects of such representations, public memory studies considers the rhetorical nature of works that address memory, and that create, shape, and reinforce cultural memory. Concerns here become kinds of memory, the means to evoke memory, the relationship between primary, personal memory and the secondary memories works about the past can represent, and the ethics of recovering and representing memory for diverse audiences.[15]

Docudrama, as a contributor to public memory, argues then not about the past as it "was," but poses propositions about how people and events should be remembered. Through the mode of docudrama we view the past as performance, as purposeful action within and in response to the arenas that define actions and actors.

The arena makes evident the balance, the interrelationship of actor, action, and place. In events docudramas the contested spaces of work and politics shape the arguments that result. The events arenas showcase the intersection of personal and public space, private ambition and public consequences. War docudramas evoke the material of memory in order to recreate the visceral space of the most extreme kind of contestation. Biopics explore what I will term "compulsive" space, the space of lives driven by the compulsions that create artists, musicians, writers, politicians, criminals, and public figures. Each arena operates as a submode, a variety, of docudramatic argument, however each arena also argues about the moral value of the contestation it showcases.

To illustrate, Oliver Stone's *Nixon* (1995), a biopic, and Ron Howard's *Frost/Nixon* (2009), an events docudrama, share not only the same subject, but also the strategy that where actions and events occur inflects how we read each film's performance of "Nixon." Both films reach the climax of their re-creation in houses, the White House in *Nixon*, and a private home in *Frost/Nixon* where the interviews that are the subject of the film will occur. The White House in *Nixon* allows us to see the subject of the biopic as simultaneously trapped and driven. The offices, meeting rooms, and bedrooms of the White House define the role, remind the President of who he is, and also of what he will lose. Frequent cut-aways during scenes in these locales to numerous documentary or documentary-like flashes of public events (war; war protests) or Nixon's family connect his behavior to his thoughts, memories, and fears. The White House as an arena allows us to understand how Nixon is compelled to grapple with past influences as a means to manage the pressures of the present. The house in *Frost/Nixon*, on the other hand, frames the unfolding event for us as it stages a contest of the present in which the personal ambitions of interviewer and interviewee take on the most public kind of consequences. It is to be a conversation with "no holds barred," displays the culmination of the desires of both men to be victors in public, while they sit, almost knee to knee, in a setting that anticipates where the product of their contest will find its audience.

The case studies in this book provide guides to the arenas within which docudrama performs the past. By no means can they document them completely and comprehensively. The broad arena of noteworthy events in this overview includes docudramas set within the spheres of work and politics. Clint Eastwood's *Changeling* (2008) will lead off this discussion since the film's "true story" showcases a collision between the two spheres. The arenas of events in *Changeling* pit personal space and memory against social institutions—law enforcement and mental health—in performing the vindication of a working mother's true memory. In *The Perfect Storm* (W. Peterson, 2000) the very scale of contestation in the work the film shows argues for the need for public memory. Work, the consequences of ambition, and the noteworthy events that result similarly drive the arguments forwarded in *Erin Brockovich* (S. Soderbergh, 2000) and *Pirates of Silicon Valley* (M. Burke, 1999). Both suggest we remember the work of their principal characters as necessary and memorable precisely as a measure of response to the power of the forces that would oppose and constrain it. The story of *Seabiscuit* (G. Ross, 2003) recovers exemplary public memory in order to equate work with cultural identity.

The case studies in docudramas about political events illuminate the codes and constraints that govern political action. Each story clarifies how the very reason for being of political process stems from the intersection of private ambition, public action, and the public knowledge and memory that result. *Strange Justice* (E. Dickerson, 1999) theatricalizes the crucible of a Senate committee hearing room in re-creating the epic confrontation between Clarence Thomas and Anita Hill. We see in the most personal terms how the left and right of American politics of the early nineties became polarized over the issues of race and gender raised by Thomas's nomination to the United States Supreme Court. As a very different film telling a vastly different story, Paul Greengrass's *United 93* (2006) also sets its story within personal, desperately contested space, as a means of making accessible the political consequences we know, and the personal consequences we can only imagine in the hijacking of the only 9/11 airliner that failed to reach its target.

The events of war constitute a second, distinct arena within which docudramas perform the past, drawing upon the material of personal memory as a means to argue for and shape public memory of people, actions, and their consequences. Within the range of eras and conflicts these films re-create, including World War II (*Defiance*; *Flags of Our Fathers*; *Uprising*; *The Pianist*; *Nuremberg*); Vietnam (*We Were Soldiers*); incursions of the 90s (*Black Hawk Down*); and Iraq (*Saving Jessica Lynch*) war docudramas perform the material of personal memory within the most visceral kinds of arenas. *Defiance* (E. Zwick, 2008) foregrounds its forest setting in order to argue for a revised public memory of Jewish resistance during the Holocaust. *Flags of Our Fathers* offers us literally a meditation on memory, as it explores the clash of various (and various kinds of) personal memories with the creation of public memory. If memory allows the past to become present, the essays that follow examine the functions and implications of that presence. *Uprising* (J. Avnet, 2001), *Nuremberg* (Y. Simoneau, 2000), and *The Pianist* (R. Polanski, 2002) focus on the physical features of setting to recover a sense of the emotional experience of the Holocaust. *Black Hawk Down* (R. Scott, 2001) and *We Were Soldiers* (R. Wallace, 2002) similarly evoke the visceral experience of combat as the premise for their arguments about the meaning of those wars. As an adaptation of historian Stephen Ambrose's printed oral history, the interviews that frame the ten episodes of *Band of Brothers* (S. Spielberg, 2001) ground re-creation to living memory in the miniseries's systematic effort to reclaim for public memory the rapidly disappearing personal histories of World War II veterans. The last entry into the arena of the events of war this section considers, *Saving Jessica Lynch* (P. Markle, 2003), returns us to the kinds of forces that influence public memory explored in *Flags of Our Fathers*. The shaping of the Jessica Lynch story echoes eerily, but not surprisingly, the construction of the war in Iraq in general.

Biopics, films that re-create the lives of noteworthy individuals, form the third and perhaps most sprawling arena of docudramatic argument. The essays here purport only to survey the topography of a terrain that includes films about musicians (*Ray*; *Walk the Line*), scientists (*Kinsey*; *A Beautiful Mind*), artists (*Pollock*; *Frida*), writers (*Capote*; *Finding Neverland*), actors (*Autofocus*; *The Life and Death of Peter Sellers*), athletes (*Cinderella Man*; *The Greatest Game Ever Played*; *The Blind Side*), criminals (*Catch Me If You Can*; *Monster*; *American Gangster*), politicians (*The Last Kind of Scotland*; *Charlie Wilson's War*; *Milk*), and public figures (*The Aviator*; *Amelia*; *Good Night, and Good Luck*). The arena of re-creation spins a common thread among these diverse stories through the recurring argument that noteworthy figures become compelled to their accomplishments because of the clash between the predispositions of their desires, ambitions, talents, and/or inclinations, and internal and external constraints that shape those desires. The brief discussions included here on a number of these, with particular attention to *Ray* (T. Hackford, 2004), *The Greatest Game Ever Played* (B. Paxton, 2005), *Bobby Jones: Stroke of Genius* (R. Herrington, 2004), and *Good Night, and Good Luck* (G. Clooney, 2005), detail how these films argue that accomplishment in these cases is a response to internal and external constraints.

The chapters that follow examine the spectrum of arguments docudramas offer as their re-creations reason from the arenas of important events, the events of war, and the lives of noteworthy individuals. The case studies show how docudrama's re-creation of "true stories," its performance of memory, warrants the claims it forwards about how to remember the past. The aggregate of examining works made since the late 1990s allows us to see how, as recurring contexts, the arenas of docudramatic argument ground action and identity in the settings that frame performance, structure the moral value of the contestation that ensues, and shape the public memory of the past that docudramas perform.

CHAPTER TWO

CHANGELING AND THE PERFORMANCE OF TRUE MEMORY

"I had one rule when I set out to write the script on this, which was that everything had to be true. I'm not saying every single line was exactly true but every scene had to have happened and not necessarily in the way that I arranged them, but there had to be the facsimile of reality, as opposed to reality itself, which of course you can never get, even if you're doing a documentary. But there has to be this kind of verisimilitude, which not only appears to be real, every scene is based on reality."
—Martyn Burke, Writer/Director, *Pirates of Silicon Valley*[16]

Clint Eastwood's 2008 *Changeling* claims, in contrast to most docudramas that are "based on a true story" to be, in fact, "a true story." The truth of *Changeling's* "true story" rests in the film's performance of the fact of memory. Performance is central in the film. Performance frames the contesting truth claims that create the fabric of *Changeling's* narrative. The film visualizes memory through the performance of role actions and behavior. The performance of roles within the film's story distinguishes between true and false memory. The performance framework associates truthful memory with actual, lived memory, and opposes this to socially pressured, assumed role performances and the fabricated memories that define them. "Truth" comes to reside in the fact of memory, the memory of people and events that we have seen, and consequently know as "fact." In line with other films Eastwood has made over the last two decades, *Changeling* also links truth in the performance of memory to survivor guilt, so that the interplay of guilt and memory form the truth of *Changeling's* "true story."

Memory offers us a performance of the past. Docudrama's performance of the past claims to re-create actual people, places, and events. The roots of the story's performance in the material of the past warrants the claims the film would forward.

"Performance" in general refers to role actions and behaviors. Both theatrical and sociological views of performance note the importance as well of the settings in which role actions occur. Sociologically, where we are impacts how we behave.[17] The performance of roles in the theater necessarily frames character behavior and action within the general setting of the theater's stage, and the more particular settings a work specifies. To view and so understand "performance" means looking at the balance, the interrelationship between action and setting. If we interpret who people are not only on the basis of what they do but where they do it (or, to rephrase, where we are frames what we do) then it is fair to say that setting and role actions are reciprocally legible. The one informs the way we read the other, and vice-versa.

Before considering how *Changeling* argues for the truth of lived memory I would like to consider how docudrama's performance of the past allows us to understand memory itself as performance. A "memory" may be an effort to recover the past, but understanding how memory stages action and events within the settings of the past reminds us how the process of memory forms instrumentally the search for truth.

Performing Memory

Docudramas, films and movies-of-the-week based on true stories, tend to find the material of their stories in the lives of noteworthy individuals or in historically important events. Docudrama's representation of its real-life subject matter immediately raises at least two basic questions: is the work true to its subject, and is its representation through the codes and conventions of feature film narrative cinema appropriate? One answer to both questions begins here from the assumption that docudramas do not claim to be documentaries, and that docudrama provides a view or a version of the past, rather than "the" history of the events and figures it represents. What docudramas do offer, from their "basis" in "true stories," is a performance of their real-life subjects.

Docudramas about significant events become a performance of both history and memory. Performance in events docudramas foregrounds memory in various ways. In doing so these works argue for a view of history *as* memory. *Changeling's* true story, for example, could proceed equally as a history of corruption in the Los Angeles Police Department

(LAPD), the muckraking work of radio evangelism in the late 1920s, or the reform of abuses in government-run mental institutions, but emphasizes instead the story of a power struggle between the forces that form individual and public memory. Re-creation, the performance of actual people and events, allows a re-imagining and re-experiencing of the past. Docudramas provide not only a performance of past events, but also an argument through re-creation that history becomes accessible not so much as static "fact" as it does as a process of remembering.

What follows will first outline the nature of performance in docudrama. I will consider performance to stem from the interrelationship of role behavior and setting, and that the various means of highlighting this interdependence in docudrama allows the mode to claim status historiographically, rather than to purport to provide documentary historical record. *Changeling* illustrates how events docudramas foreground their performance of the past as a means to argue for the importance of understanding history as the process of remembering.

Performance in Docudrama

Recent studies of acting in film have drawn on traditional, theatre-based theory to focus on what gives a performance a distinct presence on screen.[18] Areas of concern include the relationship of character and technique, and the differences between character and star acting. I wish to add to this discussion some thoughts on what is important about performance in docudrama. Docudrama narratives perform—represent—their real-life subjects by re-creating people and events. In earlier work I discussed several basic means by which docudrama legitimates, or warrants its re-creation of the real, including sequencing documentary and re-created footage, having actual real-life principals and locations share screen space to interact with re-creation, and modeling or replicating the real.[19] Docudramatic performance provides us with a model of its subject. In semiotic terms, the modeled performance in docudrama is indexically iconic. It works as a model because its resemblance is motivated directly by its real-life subjects. Much in the way that any model works, the modeling that warrants docudramatic performance offers a sense of access to, control over, perspective on, and ultimately understanding of its subject.

Modeling depends upon resemblance; the work of modeling in docudrama depends upon resemblance in both the action and the setting that constitute "performance." Performance in general is purposeful action. It is role behavior within a context that gives its action meaning.

In docudrama, modeling defines the interdependence of role action and setting. We read the one in terms of the other in order for modeling to work. The legibility of action and setting becomes reciprocal. The modeled reciprocal legibility of action and context argues for the validity and authenticity of docudramatic performance.

Setting assumes a particular importance in events docudramas, since their very choice of a subject argues for historical importance of place, time, and action. Performance in events docudramas appears as modeled action within contested space.[20] Space does not simply frame action by providing the staging ground. Space inflects action, and makes legible the codes that indicate its issues and uncertainties. Drama arises not only from the conflict of the desires of the performers, but also inheres within the contestation the space itself creates, whether it is the natural environment (*Erin Brockovich*; *A Civil Action*; *The Perfect Storm*), or the intersection of social and political forces (the streets of Derry in Greengrass's *Bloody Sunday*; the airwaves in *Good Night, and Good Luck*; the cabin of United 93; the ears of Congress in *Charlie Wilson's War*). Watching events re-created in contested space is much like a trip to an arena or coliseum, in which staging reflects the roles and functions of competitors. Contested space associates physical and ideological conflict; action based on contestation makes visible the meanings—the codes and values—at issue.

At the same time, re-creation in docudrama foregrounds its status as performance. Docudrama indicates its performance of the real in several ways. The fact that docudramas are produced, distributed, marketed, and exhibited as feature films underlines their function as entertainment products. This is performance as branded commodity. Docudramas assert that they are "based on" true stories, foregrounding their project to re-create known figures and events. Further, just as docudramas tend to signpost their status as hybrid narratives (stories—conventional narratives—incorporating "true," documentary materials), they also foreground the performances they offer as performance when, for example: *World Trade Center* (O. Stone, 2006) casts a star, Nicholas Cage, as John McLaughlin, the New York City firefighter who endured the events the film depicts; when Tom Hanks appears before us as congressman Charlie Wilson; when Philip Seymour Hoffman embodies a young Truman Capote; when Russell Crowe plays the roles of a tobacco insider, a Nobel-winning scientist, a New York City detective, or a Depression-era boxer; and when Denzel Washington reminds us of the fire of Malcolm X, the trials faced by Hurricane Carter, or the help that redefines the sense of possibility for the likes of an Antwone Fisher or talented university debaters.

Docudrama's very acknowledgement of its work as performance argues that we should view its modeling of the past historiographically, as a form of representing history, rather than as a representation of historical fact. If we accept this view of the mode, the key question becomes, not "was this what happened?" so much as, in what way(s) does performance in docudrama allow us to understand the significant people and events of the past? What is there in its modeling, its strategies of re-creation, that brings the past to life affording some new understanding of it for a viewer in the present? Robert Rosenstone suggests that "the past on screen is not meant to be literal (is history on the page?), but suggestive, symbolic, metaphoric."[21] Considering docudrama historiographically prompts asking, what does its performance of the past do?

Before turning to how *Changeling* performs the past as it exists in memory, I would like to suggest that historiography attunes us to thinking about history as diverse, sometimes even competing versions of the past. Differences in accounts render accuracy as uncertain, perpetually subject to debate. Historiographers such as Hayden White and Robert Rosenstone argue that our sense of the past becomes formed not only by comparing and contrasting these various views, but also by considering what materials are brought together and how in forming the view of the past that any particular work forwards.

If how we formulate the past brings it to life, then the performance of the past adds another consideration as to "where" the past resides. "History" is in records of the past, but it is also in memory. Since docudramas do not purport to be historical records but instead, representations of the past that perform history, it is not surprising to find that events docudramas often focus their performance of history by replicating, directly or indirectly, the process of remembering the past. One implication of evoking the past through performance that models the process of memory is that one need not have lived the past and now remembers it; a viewer can understand that what is being represented is a model of what the experience of memory does to evoke the past. Flashback structures (*Walk the Line*; *World Trade Center*; *Charlie Wilson's War*; *A Mighty Heart*) are one means to situate the events unfolding on screen within memory. Another, equally conventional strategy, is for a work to argue that key, iconic images become the images of memory, and thus of history. *Good Night, and Good Luck* builds its evocation of Edward R. Murrow's courage under fire upon its replication of the "look" of fifties television and Murrow's *See It Now* in particular. *Charlie Wilson's War* depicts the seed of its story taking root in Dan Rather's report on freedom fighters in Afghanistan on *Sixty Minutes*.

United 93 places the images of planes penetrating the World Trade Center and the collapse of the towers on screens viewed by various air traffic controllers. *Flags of Our Fathers* explores not only what might be important about a widely shared image, but also what its repercussions were, and ultimately why it is important to foreground through performance the effect on the present of memory's evocation of the past.[22] In all cases images audiences viewed became iconographic. These docudramas evoke the past, bring it life, by performing, through these key images, the very process of remembering itself.

Signposted then as a view or version of history, docudramatic performance foregrounds not only what evokes memory, but also the phenomenon of memory itself. Perhaps what the performance of the past in docudrama presumes most strongly is the need to remember, and that above all else warrants how its telling of "true stories" brings the past to life.

The Performance of Memory in *Changeling*

Changeling opposes true to false memory by presenting the differences between role actions in private and public places. Both kinds of settings function as arenas within which to stage the conflict in the story between true and false memory, and so between the actual, "natural" relationship between mother and son, and the fabricated, socially forced relationship the process of child abduction and return creates. Scenes in the privacy of the Collins home present us with the fact of the biological son and the fact of "true," lived memory. Scenes in public places—the train station, and in courtrooms—foreground the performance of memory in general, and the implications of acting out the fact of memory when one has been forced to assume a memory of the past. The foregrounding of the performance of false memory only reinforces what we know to be the truth. We know it because we and Mrs. Collins (Angelina Jolie) have seen it, and we, too, remember it.

In each of the scenes that contrast true and false memory, the space of the setting foregrounds roles, and the action we see within that space foregrounds the fact, the visual presence, of memory. The first scene occurs within the Collins home. She has promised her son that they will spend the day together and see a movie. She is called to work to fill in and so must break her promise. She explains, makes her son a sandwich that he can have later for lunch, dresses for work, and leaves. He is on his own. The scene reinforces her conflicting responsibilities as mother and provider. She is good at her job, and a reliable, competent worker. As a single, working mother she needs her job. She provides a comfortable home in a middle-class neighborhood for her son and puts food on the table. She would be the best mother she can be in the time that job responsibilities allow. She has made her son a promise, however, and the process of changing the plan, of dressing for work, packing the lunch, and leaving the house plant the seeds for the sense of guilt that will overtake her life when she returns and finds him missing.

In addition to the actions that establish role conflict (mother's promise as opposed to employee's obligation; dressed for a day off as opposed to a day of work; eating together at home as opposed to the "working" lunch) the construction of space in the scene serves to foreground the presence of the boy when she leaves, compared to his absence when she returns. He (and so their relationship) fills the kitchen. The kitchen frames the role conflicts. The kitchen provides the staging ground to show conflict inherent in the role of mother as provider, and son as dependent. The shot as she leaves shows the house's living room, pulls away from Walter framed in the window and recedes down the street beyond, suggesting the tenuous nature of the shelter from the outside the house provides.

The influence of the space outside the house, and by implication the outer world that will impinge on the relationship between mother and son, becomes reiterated when she returns home. The scene bookends the earlier departure for work. We track to the front door and see her enter from the outside. He is not there, not in the empty living room, bedroom, nor the kitchen. It is now the end of the day, and the sandwich he should have eaten for lunch remains untouched. She runs outside and searches the neighborhood for her missing son.

The son's absence becomes the visual indication of failure: failure to provide, to keep him safe, to preserve, ultimately, the relationship between mother and son. His absence indicates how her role conflict has led to her failure to fulfill her role. His absence combined with the fruitlessness of her search efforts (now and subsequently, over decades) further indicate the burden of guilt the memory of her son in the house imposes upon her.

The interplay of absence, presence, memory, setting, role behavior that setting demands, role obligation, and truth becomes foregrounded again during the scene at the train station when mother is to reunite with her discovered and recovered abducted son. Society has intervened in the mother's dilemma in the form of LAPD Captain Jones (Jeffrey Donovan), who earlier had come to her with the news of the likely discovery of her son in another state. The moment of reunion has been further set up by the prominence the investigation has received in the press, and the attention the practices and policies of the LAPD has received in the newspapers and through the muckraking efforts of a popular radio minister. There is tremendous social pressure on the police to perform, and so the moment of reunion is equally a moment of vindication for the police. Consequently the reunion is a highly public moment. The train station is thronged with the press and curious onlookers. It is a stage set to frame the performances of cop and mother.

The boy who is supposed to be her son is brought off the train. His appearance fills the absence marked by the empty house and the fruitless search. However, immediately both she and we can see that this child resembles her son, but is different—it is not him. His presence to fulfill the role of her biological son is a lie.

She tells this to the detective, and he pulls her aside. He creates a private moment in this highly public space. Time has passed, he suggests; likely the boy has grown and changed given the passage of time, the misadventures he has endured; perhaps, he implies, her memory deceives her. Further, he emphasizes the public nature of the moment. They must accept this child as hers, at least here, in public view.

Her acceptance of his suggestions indicates the weight of social pressure, visible in the presence of the cop and the presence of the public, to bend what a mother knows to be the truth. She is forced to assume a role and with it the lie of both the fact of who her son is, and just as important, her memory of her son. She and we know, however, that the truth is rooted in our memories of the visible evidence of her biological child, and it is this knowledge, this truth, the fact of memory, that drives the rest of her story.

She is forced to take him home and treat him as her own. He says little. When she bathes him, and confronts him with the fact that he is circumcised and her son was not, he continues to say nothing, but to call her his mother. The collision of role performance, the fact of memory, and the forced falsehood of social pressure recurs when she tries to point out to a physician that this child has been circumcised, and his response is much like what we've heard before, that this was probably part of the boy's mistreatment during his abduction. Social pressure continues to intervene in denying the fact of a mother's memory.

Though an entirely different story from Eastwood's earlier *Flags of Our Fathers*, *Changeling* similarly pins much of the truth of its true story on the performance of memory. In both films performance becomes a means to meditate upon the truth of memory itself when performance allows us to understand the contrasts between kinds of memory, in particular the primary, personal memory and its associated traumas that collides with coerced, manufactured, public memory that the narrative allows us to see in the context of role behavior within contested private and public spaces.

Both *Changeling* and *Flags of our Fathers* foreground the performance of history and memory as a means to access the past. The emphasis on performance in both films acknowledges the singularity and relativity of viewpoint that forms the basis for memory. The centrality of performance in these works allows them to explore the authenticity of lived memory, and to argue that truth in memory stems from understanding the very nature of memory itself as performance.

CHAPTER THREE

TEACHING REVERENCE FOR THE REAL: CAUTIONARY VALUES IN EVENTS DOCUDRAMA

The Perfect Storm (W. Petersen, 2000) begins and ends by evoking a tour for us to a site of public memory. Close-ups track portions of a memorial wall in Gloucester, Massachusetts, allowing us to read inscribed names and dates ranging over two centuries of townspeople who have lost their lives working upon the sea. The images frame appropriately our entrance to and exit from the arena that forms the world of the work of the swordfishermen, the forces of contestation that drive their work, and the film itself as a performance of their memory.

With their basis in "true stories" docudramas invariably point us toward the previously known. They invite us to compare the film we are watching to the state of public memory, the images and impressions we hold of the previously known actions, events, people, and texts that are the stuff of the story. Docudramas adapt and shape the material they reference.

Reviewers at the time of the release of *The Perfect Storm* viewed the film as a failed adaptation of what they considered praiseworthy in Sebastian Junger's best-selling book. Junger's work of "scrupulous" nonfiction[23] offered a study of the "history of fishing"[24] as well as "seamanship and weather"[25] that was thorough, riveting, knowledgeable, even philosophical. Petersen's film, on the other hand, sacrificed these values for the sake of corporately mandated special effects,[26] "muffed" romance,[27] and sketchy character development.[28] Richard Corliss perhaps encapsulated critical opinion most succinctly when he wrote, "it's not a bad movie, except for the people."[29] We are offered, instead, an "interminable deluge of effects"[30] showing "100-ft. waves tossing boats like rubber ducks in a bathtub"[31] with George Clooney "shouting interminably while two or three guys off camera chuck buckets of water in his face."[32] Stuart Klawans began his review in *The Nation* with the words, "long before I'd gone to a theater and lashed myself to a seat ..."[33]

These reviews give lengthy attention to the film's measures to show the extremes of nature that set the story and drive its plot. Critics' concern for the film's special effects suggests, alternatively, that the film directed the energy of its adaptation into depicting cinematically what was most substantial in Junger's book, weather and its effects on the people in this story. Both the book and the film, in varying ways appropriate to the strengths of each medium, emphasize nature and the size of the opposition that it poses to human efforts to work with and within it.

As a docudrama, Petersen's *The Perfect Storm* centers on the relationship between human work and forces of nature. It frames its argument about this relationship through a Quixote-like metaphor of a hero facing insurmountable opposition because he has been driven to the point of delusion by a goal. Through this metaphor the film argues that work and our response to it are both necessary, even immutable. The film's docudramatization of Junger's material offers a simultaneously affirmative, reverential, and yet critical view of work. The film affirms work as a necessary grappling with nature in order to survive. Even as it does so it criticizes that work as exploitative and victimizing. Much as Junger's book does, the film shows us that in this line of work the materiality—the reality—of high risk and great effort must be counterbalanced by the ideal of reward. Both works admire and question the necessity of the equation.

The reviews of the film also comment at length on the element of masculinity in the film's presentation of work. "Manly competence" characterizes the fishermen as well as the Coast Guard rescuers.[34] The groups of dedicated professionals in both arenas evoke images reminiscent of Howard Hawks films.[35] Klawans notes bluntly that the film "not only resexualizes the world of work but oversexualizes it."[36] Is the characterization too strong? Certainly images of boathooks pulling in swordfish, or Captain Billy Tyne (Clooney) mounted on the boom trying to cut the chain of a flailing stabilizer, cross-cut with the rescue helicopter's re-fueling rod angling in mid-air to seat itself in the cup of the tanker jet's supply hose would tend to confirm it.

It is equally valid to think of these as images of tilting at the windmills of the opposition, indicating the effort necessary in this work to struggle against the overwhelming opposing forces of nature. Much like the *Man of La Mancha* version of the story, this Don Quixote also depends upon his noble steed (the Andrea Gail, his ship), his trustworthy Sancho-like companion (Bobby), the validation of his Dulcinea (Linda), and the righteousness of his impossible dream, which, in this case, is to "bring home a shitload of fish." Similarly, Billy's desire to follow his (and his crew's) dreams isolates him. Corliss notes, appropriately, that "Billy could be his own Bogart festival. At first he is the grizzled boat captain in *To Have and Have Not*; then he's greedy Fred C. Dobbs in *The Treasure of the Sierra Madre*, risking his mates' lives to make the big score; finally, he nears the daft steeliness of *The Caine Mutiny*'s Captain Queeg."[37] As a matter of filmic adaptation of Sebastian Junger's original source material, these images offer their answer to the question of why this tragedy happened. The Quixote-like dedication to their goals of both Billy and his men, and the crew of the Coast Guard rescue helicopter, becomes legible in the film as a loss of perspective for the sake of attaining ideals.

The film defines heroic action as warranted effort, action that is responsible when it is devoted to work. In this sense *Storm* offers a traditionally existential view of heroism that situates individual effort within systems that define it. One function of the film's Quixote metaphor is to validate the nobility of individual effort as it tilts against the "windmill" of not simply nature, but also the social systems that put men at work with nature. These systems include: jobs and the responsible, authentic actions that fulfill work responsibilities; family responsibilities and expectations; and community as a platform for both.

The film characterizes the work of swordfishing by suggesting that quantity—of fish, of profits, and of property—has precedence over people involved and their risk of death. Billy and Linda (Mary Elizabeth Mastrantonio) unload their catches along with one of Linda's crew, the body enshrouded in plastic. Bob, the owner of the two boats, seems less concerned about the dead crewman than the fact that Billy's "numbers" aren't as good as Linda's. A run of shots of the large fish carcasses with their weight marked on each one ends with Billy and Linda exchanging glances over a particularly large specimen that reiterates cinematically that hers is "bigger" than his. Work mediates their relationship. The next scene further underlines numerically the pressures of the system. Bob explains to a sailor how his paycheck has been computed. What each man earns comes after, rather than before expenses. Bob further flexes the muscle of ownership by threatening to take the Andrea Gail away from Billy if he can't do something about the "record low" return he's producing. Bob suggests Billy "track Linda, she can find the fish." When Billy responds that he'll go further to catch more, Bob tells him that he likes him, but that he "likes [his] boat better" and he wants it back. These early scenes clarify not only the terms of labor but also the stakes. People, however, define themselves by the quality of their work. The refrain is repeated a number of times in the film: they are Gloucestermen. Billy draws on the combination of masculine pride and professional motivation in their efforts to compete in the numbers game when he tells the crew that "this is the moment of truth," that they need to go to the Flemish Cap to "separate the men from the boys" or "crawl home busted."

The numbers these scenes emphasize indicate the economic constraints that characterize this work. The film's view of work also encompasses its relationship with nature through detailing the specifics of the routine of swordfishing: taking on supplies; laying out and reeling in lines and bait; hauling in and processing the catch; accidents; the pressures of living in confined spaces aboard ship contrasted with images of the vastness of the ocean; and of course, images of the size and power of the weather that the work operates within. The two "money shots" perhaps most associated with *The Perfect Storm*, the tracking shot through the cycling hurricane that ends with a wave-tossed freighter, and the penultimate shot of the Andrea Gail struggling to climb the wall of the monstrous rogue wave that turns her end to end, reiterate the size of nature's opposition compared to the mortals attempting to work within it. One analysis of the screenplay suggested that the film seeks to capture as risk the basic human need to tilt against opposition this vast:

> What drives men and some women to risk all in a hard, unforgiving, dirty, and often terrifying line of work? The answer suggested by the script is twofold: the ultimate power of the sea to trump anything humans can come up with, accounting for the death rate, but also the comparably uncontrollable fact of human nature, which will put itself at risk against all practical strictures advising caution and common sense. Sometimes this embracing of risk is driven by economic necessity; at other times it is part of a sense of identity, of how a life should be lived.[38]

The idea of refusing to do this work never arises. Perhaps more than being patriarchal, the system is ritualistic, from the specifics of the work we see on ship to the interactions that work structures for those waiting on shore. The lingering shots of the memorial wall that open and close *The Perfect Storm* not only remind, again, of the numbers at stake in this world (we learn that 10,000 from Gloucester have perished at sea over the last few hundred years) but also how the confluence of the need to work, the effort the work demands, and vast forces of nature have endured, ostensibly and essentially unchanged and unchallenged.

The Perfect Storm translates its view of work caught in the contest between natural and economic forces into its presentation of interpersonal relationships. In addition to the role conflicts Billy faces as an employee and as a competitor with another captain in this small fleet, the film emphasizes the constraints work imposes on the relationships between potential lovers (Billy and Linda; Bugsy and Irene), actual lovers (Bobby and Chris), husbands and wives (Murph and his ex), and even mothers and sons (Bobby and his mother).   The film uses the culture of work to personalize social and economic issues.   Accordingly it translates the constraints created by work into moral conflict.

The frustrated affairs of Bobby and Chris and Murph and his ex (and their son) are cases in point. Murph's work has destroyed his marriage ("it was the old times that ruined us"), and has created the need for his son to have an on-scene father.   Bobby   (Mark Wahlberg) needs a big score swordfishing because he and Chris (Diane Lane) are trying to put away enough money to "get her kids back." His work separates them physically and emotionally, as they fight about his need to leave to work. The film underlines the way that work opposes, rather than facilitates these desires in scenes near the film's opening (Chris is dreaming prophetically about Bobby in a storm) and its end, when Bobby floats adrift, his thoughts reaching out to Chris to tell her he loves her.   The romance of these devices indicates that Chris's and Bobby's desire for each other transcends physical limits. The near-telepathic link between the two frustrated lovers argues that while desire mediates, work separates, and by doing so raises questions about the work's larger purposes.

The film personalizes moral issues also when Chris confronts Bob (Michael Ironside), the boat owner, who has walked into the Crow's Nest to tell the small Gloucester community there that they've lost radio contact with the Andrea Gail.   She accuses him with, "You're counting your money, while my guy's out there risking his life." She tries to beat her fists on his chest. Beyond the moment's fusion of economics and emotion, it humanizes the economic issues that have allowed a disaster to create a crisis, and portrays Bob's role in terms of a moral dilemma. "What do you want," Chris throws at Bob when he walks in to face everyone, "credit for having the guts to walk in here?"   Clearly he's damned if he does and damned if he doesn't. An old salt looks up from his glass and urges them to "give it to him."   Bob is, if not an equal member, then at least an undeniable element of their community structure.

The scenes in the Crow's Nest, and most importantly, the memorial service that concludes *The Perfect Storm*, demonstrate how the film replaces family with images of community, and uses familial rituals to represent visually public, shared, therefore known events. This is a story about groups, both on ship and ashore. Community acts here as family. Everyone gathered at the Crow's Nest, for example, knows who is fighting with whom, who is trying to pick up whom, and, thanks to the swaying light fixtures, even who is screwing whom in the bedrooms upstairs. All relationships happen in full sight of the family/community. More than functioning melodramatically, however, the film's presentation of community space in the Crow's Nest, the town hall, and even in re-creating the Andrea Gail, anchors its docudramatic claims in public, and therefore historical space. The memorial service that concludes the film returns us visually to the film's opening, scanning the wall that lists the names of the thousands from the town who have been lost over the years, linking the material of the work of docudrama to the work that has motivated the need to tell about this subject. Sebastian Junger said of this scene:

> One of the last scenes to be filmed in Gloucester was at St. Peter's Church, where they used 700 locals to shoot a memorial service for the dead fishermen. I wasn't there but I heard about it from a lot of people, including Wolfgang Petersen. It was a strange blurring of fiction and reality, he said, one of the most intense experiences he'd ever had on set. During a eulogy given by the actress Mary Elizabeth Mastrantonio, whole sections of the audience started to cry, including family and friends of the original crew. They'd sat in the same church eight years earlier, listening to virtually the same words.[39]

Appropriately, the film ends in ritual. The rituals of work, separation, confrontation, and mourning create the social fabric here, and like all rituals, reinforce the enduring nature of the forces acting in concert to create these events. The community configurations throughout the film, the closing re-creation of Gloucester paying its last respects once more to those it has lost, or the more informal town meetings we see periodically in the Crow's Nest, all consequently contribute their share to the representation in the film that simultaneously presents, critiques, and affirms the social systems that constrain the characters of the story.

The ritual of community action in the film shows the very Quixote-like nature of man's necessary struggle with a vast opposition as ongoing. Thus the *Perfect Storm* story can at once critique the institutions that have formed around and sustain the work of swordfishing, and at the same time affirm the continuing struggles the work necessitates. We may see the work of fishing, the roles it creates, and the economy and institutions that support it as wrong in the ratio of risk and reward that result, but we also see it equally as embedded within this enduring struggle. This is the source of the film's affirmative critique of its subject.

The Perfect Storm's epic opposition of human desire and natural forces exemplifies a strategy of fusing nature and human institutions that runs across many feature film docudramas released around 2000. What replaces the "windmill" of opposition posed by a work system bound by the forces of nature in *The Perfect Storm* has a counterpart in the coupling of environmental issues and the court system in *Erin Brockovich* (S. Soderbergh, 1999) and *A Civil Action* (S. Zaillian, 1999), and/or health issues and the court system in *Patch Adams* (T. Shadyac, 1998) and *The Insider* (M. Mann, 1999).   Other docudramas also pit an idealistic protagonist against a monumentally opposing social system (courts again in *The Hurricane* [N. Jewison, 1999]; the military in *Men of Honor* [G. Tillman, 2000]; arenas of competition in *October Sky* [J. Johnston, 1999], *Thirteen Days* [R. Donaldson, 2000], and *Remember the Titans* [B. Yakin, 2000]).   In all cases, the inherent drama, anchored in actuality, asks us to accept the terms of struggle as necessary, affirming the shortcomings of institutions in the very spectacle of the struggle and vindication of the idealists whose stories now contribute to public memory.

CHAPTER FOUR

WHEN THE PRIVATE BECOMES PUBLIC: FILM AND TV EVENTS DOCUDRAMAS SET THE RECORD STRAIGHT

A title "based on a true story" promises, at least implicitly, that we will have a chance to see what occurred privately, behind the scenes, while events unfolded in public view. Docudramas set within the arenas of events, diverse as they are in subject matter, not surprisingly then tell a recurring kind of story: the profound ambitions of a story's real-life principal(s) confront and so serve to illuminate varied matters of work, family, law, politics, and social issues. Films as different as *Men of Honor* (G. Tillman, 2000), *A Mighty Heart* (M. Winterbottom, 2007) and *The Great Debaters* (D. Washington, 2007) share this basic narrative purpose. Events in this arena occur often because of work. Work here, as it often does in the biopic, offers an accessible site from which to explore the intersection of personal ambitions and public consequences. As the case of *The Perfect Storm* suggests, work provides the material of cautionary tales, as it demonstrates for us the ambitions of those creating and affected by events. Films and movies-of-the-week in the events arena explore equally the benefits and the costs of ambition for their main characters, their families, and their communities. The resulting stories that view events as the consequences of ambition contribute to the processes of shaping public memory and cultural identity. The stories argue that redemption is warranted, not only by the actual events that motivate their telling, but also through the physical, temporal, and spatial components of the arenas that frame the narrative. In the vein of cautionary tales, events docudramas argue that the desire for self-determination fuels ambition, and the rituals that allow for and demonstrate the redemption of ambition can be both costly and empowering.

The actual material of these works unfolds through stories of victims whose struggles to become empowered demand surviving the vicissitudes of repressive ideologies that both threaten and enable the exercise of justice. Both feature film and movie-of-the-week (MOW) modes of presentation emphasize the verdicts, that is, the moral implications the resolutions of their stories clarify. They differ fundamentally, however, in how they view the presence and functions of social systems. The differences between feature film and MOW re-presentation will be evident in how both treat the nature of victimization, how they visualize sites of conflict, and how their treatment of family, peers, and community allows truth claims.

To explore these points of comparison this chapter will examine *Erin Brockovich* (S. Soderbergh, 2000), a theatrically distributed feature film. It will invite in the chapter that follows comparisons to *Pirates of Silicon Valley* (M. Burke, 1999), a telefeature. The comparison builds on traditional distinctions between large and small screen representation. It suggests that the potentially self-destructive ambitions of the central characters in features are directed "away" from themselves as a means to focus on a larger community of victims. The energy of explanation moves "inward" in the telefeature narrative; here ambition becomes a means to explore the vulnerabilities created by individual personality. The emphatic presence of community in feature film narratives at moments of resolution links the claims of the story to public record and larger "truth," while the telefeatures focus on making accessible the "inside" knowledge of family and peers.

Erin Brockovich and *Pirates of Silicon Valley* exemplify the larger argument that self-actualization results from and is a counterforce to corporate/patriarchal repression. Ambition here, as well, as we will see, in the biopic, victimizes as well as empowers main characters. The discussion later in this book of *Strange Justice* (E. Dickerson, 2000) provides a further case study in how the public repercussions of private ambition not only impacts public memory, but also drives the clash of values underpinning legal, political, and cultural conflict. When conflicts growing out of the ideological constraints evident within legal and corporate systems place the aspirations of the people whose stories we're watching on "trial" their respective abilities to persist, to tilt against a repressive opposition is witnessed—and because it is seen, validated—by family, peers, community, and audience, both on-screen and off. As a result both the telefeature and feature filmic modes of representation equate the respective spectator positions they develop with docudramatic public knowledge and would contribute accordingly to public memory.

Erin Brockovich: **From the Personal to the Public**

The confluence of character and star in *Erin Brockovich* (*EB*) allows the film to offer its own particular spin on how docudrama strikes the balance between personal and public history. As do other MOW and feature film docudramas, *EB* traces the process of how the personal shifts into the realm of the public when victims become witnesses and find the means to articulate their grievances. More particularly, *EB* links articulation, finding the effective expression of what victims must say and the means they have to say it, to public events and so, by implication, public knowledge. The film creates this link by centering on spectatorship and progressively inscribing the processes of spectatorship it creates within community presence. Janet Staiger has suggested that a docudrama invites us to construct hypotheses about the verisimilitude of the text, the relations between story processes and real world.[40]   *EB* compounds its claims regarding the verisimilitude of its re-creation when it depicts an actual, public event (the Hinckley town meeting to enlist the residents' participation in a class action suit) and structures its re-creation through the action of witnessing what occurred. By doing so the film builds its argument upon a premise that Staiger terms the "ideology of the visible,"[41] anchoring its claims in re-creating the process of what it was like to be a spectator in a community event. Re-created public events that become venues for articulating testimony and verdicts recur regularly in events docudramas and biopics in the form of trials (*The Hurricane*; *Patch Adams*), performances (*Music of the Heart*; *Shine*), and public gatherings (*The Perfect Storm*; *Rosewood*). Not surprisingly, it is the interdependence of character and star that allow the film to forward its claims for docudramatic truth through depicting the transformation of what would otherwise have remained hidden, private harms into public, spectatorial events.

While on the one hand, star casting raises questions about the strength of docudramatic re-creation (how proximate to the real-life principal are the images we're offered? is the dual reading created by star as character a strength or a distraction?), on the other hand, in this case there is little question that it allows the film to use the experience of spectatorship it offers to mount its arguments about its subject. Whether or not they gave *EB* a "thumbs up" or a "thumbs down," critics reviewing the film when it was released agreed unanimously that Julia Roberts's Erin Brockovich is the visual nucleus of the film. The reviews indicate not only the importance of the presence Roberts gives the character, but also agree on how that character functions consistently to direct the gaze of the film's

spectator.   One reviewer wrote, "she is in every scene, and it's her
response to events, her personal growth and (to use the current term)
empowerment that we observe."[42] Beyond mere ubiquity, Roberts's star
turn gives the character a photogenetic magnetism:

> In an instructive two-shot, Roberts sits screen right beside the old pro
> Finney, a crack shot with any line reading. As he speaks, Roberts looks
> intently off screen. Your eyes lock on her face. Finney could set himself
> on fire, and you would not look away [...] at once glamorous (celestial)
> and tangible (down to earth) Roberts satisfies the eye of all beholders.
> Men want her; women want to be like her; men are at ease with her;
> women do not resent her.[43]

The real/ideal magnetism of the desire to witness Roberts's Erin
Brockovich derives power from two sources: the star, of course, is
inflecting character, however, the role itself is warranted as the
docudramatic re-creation of a real-life principal.[44] Roberts's Erin is our
primary visual reference for the film's presentation of victims, the trials
they undergo in their efforts to act as witnesses, and the articulation of
what those trials mean.   In forwarding this argument the film positions
Erin as both victim and, through her role as mother, allows her to act
effectively as the agent for other victims.

Erin's ambition to help the residents of Hinkley grows out of her own
victimization. Joining the main characters of other feature film docudramas,[45]
Erin becomes potentially a victim of her own ambition.   Both *EB* and
Pirates root ambition in the experiences of the main characters as victims.
Ambition creates victims. From its very first scenes, *EB* establishes that
motherhood mediates ambition and victimization.   Over the opening
credits we watch Erin interviewing for jobs, trying to convert managerial
experience as a single mother into spunky, but ineffective arguments for
professional job skills. The film's opening also establishes that Erin is ill-
served by the courts.   While the credits continue the montage moves
briskly to Erin's testimony at the personal injury lawsuit she is bringing
against an ER doctor we've seen only a few shots earlier run a red light
and viciously broadside her little sedan. All she wants, she says under
oath (as well as cervical collar), is "to be a good mom" and "a good
person."   The suggestion by opposing counsel that as a several-times
divorced, single mother her habitual irresponsibility may have made her,
in fact, responsible for the accident, leads to an explosion of expletives
that, like her clothing, is a basic part of Erin's entire package

As the opening credits end (Erin wearily arriving home, holding her
crying infant while trying to open a can of something that will become

dinner for her and her three children) the film has put all of its basic ironies in place. Similar to Mrs. Collins in *Changeling*, Erin somehow has to reconcile the dilemma facing any parent who works: she needs to work, but she also needs to be a mother. Moreover, she wants to work, but has lost her job (being a waitress) due to her injury. The irony of her situation, that she has become injured while trying to find a better job, can't receive compensation for her injury through the courts, and can't, for the time being, find a new job because she is injured, only emphasizes the potential for victimization caused by the conflicting responsibilities inherent within the role of a working single mother.

Her dilemma only becomes clearer when she creates a job for herself (legal investigator), becoming so good at what she does that work comes to consume almost all of her time and energy. One review of the film noted that "even though Erin begins the picture by talking about her children, even though she's shown making sacrifices for them (including going hungry), she is capable of neglecting the kids, once she's found paying work and an outlet for a formidable energy.[46] By absenting herself but finally providing for her children is she still being the "good mom" she wants to be? Erin's job partially allows her to bring together her desires to work and to be a mother by figuratively "mothering" the clients she helps. The film creates a larger system of signifiers based on mothers and "motherhood." Besides Erin, the other victims in this story are the residents of Hinkley, California, who have been harmed for decades by the chemicals Pacific Gas and Electric (PG&E) has dumped in their drinking water, by the company's illegal efforts to cover up its actions, and then by the company's legal efforts to use the law to circumvent its responsibilities to its victims. The town's residents, like Erin, have been victimized by both laws and corporate values that disempower them. Most of the people of Hinkley Erin talks to are mothers or parents. The most graphic, detailed harms we see Erin learning about center, for example, on a bald, young, hollow-eyed girl undergoing chemotherapy for her leukemia (she'll "break a lot of hearts" when she's back in school, Erin notes), or Donna (Marge Helgenberger), a mother of several children close in age to Erin's, who asks Erin after they learn that despite multiple surgeries, her cancer has returned, "if you don't have any breasts or a uterus, are you still a woman?" The film shows motherhood under attack when it is mothers and children we see hurt most explicitly by PG&E. The lawsuit joins six hundred men, women, and children in their claims for damages against the company. Since Hinkley is an agricultural area crops and livestock are also affected. PG&E's contamination of Hinkley's water system and consequently the area's entire ecosystem violates mother earth, destroying the land's normal ability to sustain its own. "We had that water brought in special for you from Hinkley," Erin tells one of PG&E's attorneys reaching for a glass at the conference table. It drives home their position: how can there be an early and inadequate settlement when the earth itself has fallen victim to such wide-scale, long-term corporate greed and indifference? It becomes appropriate, then, that the character of Erin Brockovich embodies a Quixote-like mission within the persona of a mother figure. As one critic noted:

> PG&E's crime is not a violation of civil law but a sin against nature, a rape of the land. Male, scientific rationality has poisoned the nurturing soil, defiling Mother Nature and deforming her offspring. The tokens of Erin's fecundity ("They're called boobs, Ed") are the breastplate of an avenging angel, the earthy mother come to banish the despoilers and nurse her children back to health.[47]

EB's victims appear within a pattern of images that shows motherhood threatened and harmed. The victimizer(s) in the film, the legal and corporate systems that perpetuate harms, remain characterized as bland and repressive. The lawyers that represent PG&E are underlings, who make brief appearances in the film and have relatively little to say. No particular human antagonist comes to embody the actions and intentions of the company or the court system. The most specific image the film presents of PG&E is an extreme long shot of its Hinkley facility, a large brick building that squats on the distant horizon in a barren, desert landscape. Its most particular threats occur when, at one point, two anonymous PG&E hard hats chase Erin when she is collecting water samples on company property, and then later, when she receives an anonymous, threatening phone call. PG&E's real damage has occurred before the story even begins. Harm results more from process than specific action. The film even withholds the possibilities created by legal melodrama, allowing much of the legal action to occur off-screen. What the film argues, instead, is much more difficult to display: that actual and potential harm reside within institutional processes that appear to be the norm, the regular ways to proceed.

The film consistently shows that the routines through which the legal system works are repressive. The film filters this argument through Erin's experiences with the courts, her own law office, the lawyers she encounters, and the legal groundwork that occupies her. When she loses her lawsuit at the film's beginning and can't find a new job, she tries repeatedly to talk to Ed Masry (Albert Finney), her lawyer, eventually earning an audience with him by simply showing up at his office and working there, even though she's not yet been hired. The entire office staff stops and watches their conversation, a confrontation she finally wins by glancing around them and whispering, "Don't make me beg" for the job she needs. The office—her co-workers, and Ed himself—make her clothing an issue about which she refuses to compromise. When she starts researching the Hinkley matter she is fired after being absent from the office for the week she is out in the field, finding experts and witnesses. The Hinkley problem itself is suppressed in routine. Erin finds it buried in files, in correspondence and supporting documents related to real estate, rather than personal injury matters, and as with so much else in the film, it is left to her energy and persistence to bring the substance of the problem to light.

Even after Erin is accepted, on board and leading the investigation, the legal process she is supposed to be a part of is presented as threatening through its indirection and blandness. Ed takes on a partner, Kurt (Peter Coyote) to share the substantial labor the case has created, but does so without allowing Erin to partner the decision, so that she arrives at the office one day and sees the new part of the team at a distance, separate from her, through the conference room window talking to Ed, but unable to discern the words exchanged. The new female lawyer who poses a threat since she is to take over much of the work Erin has been doing by herself is a visual emblem of dehumanized legal process: she is self-effacing in the plainness of her masculine gray business suit, but worse, incompetent in her ability to relate to their clients as human beings. A moment that shows her unwilling to dirty her shoes to cross a barnyard to talk to one of their clients, shows her, in fact, unable even to call out to the man, underlines what we have seen in the nature of Erin's work all along: the chore is to bring what has been hidden out into the light, whether it has been kept in the depths of files in a law or water department office, or in the private tragedies of the victims the pollution has devastated.

Erin's ambition to work effectively for her clients, to bring the harm done to them out into the open, grows out of her own potential victimization by the legal system. Part of her ability comes from translating what has happened to her into encouraging her clients to do the same for themselves, to act by speaking out. Erin is an effective agent for her Hinkley clients since she is the living proof that victims become empowered when they act, and that their first act must be to articulate the nature of the harm that has befallen them. Rather than showcasing literal trials, the film instead emphasizes the figurative trials Erin undergoes through her efforts to gain, keep, and then fulfill work responsibilities. Erin, as a Quixote-like figure, battling the vast power and blandness of courts and corporations, becomes a means of moral clarification. Her efforts as a single, working mom without formal legal training shed light not only the insidiousness of the size and nature of the opposition, but also on the moral implications of working for a greater good despite the possible damage her devotion to the cause may be creating in taking time and energy away from her own family.

As the agent representing the other victims in this story, Erin facilitates their shift from isolated, disenfranchised, powerless individuals to participants who gain power through unified expression of their grievances and group action to rectify the harm done to them. Erin's work has two sides in accomplishing this change: it is both investigative (bringing harms and the harmed to light) and persuasive. Enabling her clients to testify and working to ensure that their statements are heard completes the larger process in the film of rectifying wrong through articulation and verdict.

Witnessing What Is Public

The film presents the transformation of victims into effective witnesses by returning to Erin herself as the center of spectatorship. The town meeting scene in *EB* creates a dual emphasis on witnessing when, finally, it brings all of its victims together in the opportunity to act as witnesses, and then positions Erin (for the only time in the film) not as an actor now so much as a witness to the culmination of her own labors. The structure of the scene equates processes of spectatorship with public knowledge, so that its presentation of both kinds of witnessing warrants the docudramatic claims of the film. In re-creating what was publicly witnessed, *EB* warrants its claims about the real by means of the visible.[48] The scene draws together several of the film's larger arguments: it defines the abstraction "class action suit" in specific terms anchored in the actuality the film references; it shows the law (and a lawyer) as capable of facilitating grievances; and finally, it shows Erin as a catalyst because she functions as a mediator between people and process, implying that this function is a logical outgrowth of the motherhood signifiers that have characterized her throughout.

The Hinkley town meeting scene is an appropriate culmination of legal processes in the film: rather than go to trial, it appears that there will be a faster, perhaps more financially effective resolution to the lawsuit if all the plaintiffs agree to an arbitration process. The purpose of the meeting is to explain this, and to give the hundreds of litigants an opportunity to sign on to the agreement. The scene forms the dramatic "high point" to the way the film depicts how legal processes work. There is no courtroom confrontation; instead, the scene focuses on Ed Masry's abilities to explain matters to his clients, showing Erin as a bystander, watching how (and if) her labors will bear fruit.

The dramatic premise creates the scene's suspense: the legal team needs the signatures if their work will be able to continue. Resentment has been growing about denying a public airing of PG&E's harms through a jury trial. Success or failure depends now on Ed's abilities as a persuasive speaker who can convince "real" people of his sincerity and his competence. Partway through the meeting, these people are unconvinced and begin to stand up to walk out. The docudramatic premise for the scene is that it re-creates an actual, public event, so that the large number of real-life principals the scene references attests to the validity of its depiction of people and events.

Ironically, *EB*'s presentation of the plaintiffs evoked the most stringent criticism leveled against the film: "In Hinkley, plenty of people are angry over *Erin*, which they feel portrays the lawyers as white knights and the townspeople as a bunch of hicks. Residents are angry because while the movie makes it seem that justice was done, in fact only 600 of the town's 1,000 residents won a money award."[49] And in the same review: "Most of us got screwed," says Lyn Morris. "We didn't know about the original lawsuit. Only a little clique knew." Whether or not 600 people is a "class" or a "little clique" the reaction the review cites attests to the basic argument the film has developed about the large number of victims, the pervasiveness of the harm done to the town, and the time and the energy necessary to bring so many of those affected together in group action. The town meeting scene warrants its claims about its subject by depicting an actual, public event, showing the large number of people who attended, but more importantly, re-creating the actuality as a spectatorial event that we, as the film's spectators, join through the perspective of the townspeople attending the meeting and Erin watching it. Throughout the film, we have been cued to watch Erin; now we are positioned to witness her as a witness to this culmination of her work.

The visual structure of the scene emphasizes witnessing. The scene establishes and reinforces the optical viewpoints of both speaker and audience. A hand-held camera alternates between shots of Ed speaking, shown from the level and eyeline of someone sitting in the audience, and reverse angle shots of the crowd, filmed from Ed's side. The combination of strategies (participatory camera; perspective of both speaker and audience) positions us in part as witnesses to the event. The space of the scene, however, also encompasses Erin's perspective as she stands off to the side watching Ed's efforts to persuade his clients that this is the best way to proceed, and the reactions building in the audience to what he is saying.

The scene's identification mechanisms are informed not only by the film's ongoing inducement to watch Erin, but also by its extension of the "mothering" metaphor that has governed Erin's relationships with nearly everyone. It has been her role to "mother" her own children, to allow them to be "mothered" by George, her boyfriend, to extend this relationship to the management of Ed, her boss, and ultimately to her Hinkley clients. The town meeting scene shows Erin watching Ed and eventually approving of his adaptation of her management style ("treat them like people"). To underline this suggestion of Erin as a managerial presence, the scene ends by cutting to Erin counting and filing the signed agreements; the cut implies cause and effect, that what preceded— showing (finally) Ed's persuasive abilities, the large boxes of documents that represent the potential for their case to succeed—has been all "for" her. The moment marks the climax of the film's legal action. What remains of the film's display of the law is largely resolution, so that the settlement of the case and dividing the proceeds validates the film's basic docudramatic argument: when victims become witnesses, when they can find effective means to articulate their grievances, when personal experience becomes public knowledge and enters public memory, then it becomes possible for justice to triumph.

CHAPTER FIVE

WAYS TO WATCH THE REAL: SPECTATORSHIP STRATEGIES IN *PIRATES OF SILICON VALLEY*

> "We were blessed in one way on this. They were known figures publicly, but not so well known. We got away with them because also there was this gap. It wasn't them as they were at that time, or as they are today, obviously. It was them at an earlier stage in their life. People didn't really know exactly what they looked like at that stage in their life. They knew a bit about it, but not a lot. And that gap of knowledge helped us to bring it off, I think."
> —Martyn Burke, director, *Pirates of Silicon Valley*[50]

In shaping public memory by bringing us works based on true stories docudramas make visible what would otherwise be inaccessible. To accomplish this docudramas such as *Changeling* and *Erin Brockovich* assert that if investigation offers knowledge, to re-create the act of investigation allows the opportunity to make that knowledge public and memorable.

As a movie-of-the-week *Pirates of Silicon Valley* (1999) claims that public knowledge can result from re-creating disclosure, the testimony or confessions of real-life principals who have had direct, authoritative access to the actuality they discuss. The "dialogue" they open with us is not only appropriate to the means of presentation, but also draws upon the abilities of televisually constructed works to relegate material to the realm of discussion. Filmic re-presentation of otherwise unavailable or inaccessible subjects and events argues that it offers its spectator a necessary form of knowledge.[51] Docudrama draws upon the potential to position us, as spectators, to believe that to the extent that we can know anything we "know" what we see. Accordingly, docudramas argue in part that forms of spectatorship become forms of public knowledge, or more specifically, a kind of knowledge based on, and circumscribed by strategies of re-presentation.

Beginning from the same kind of premise as *Erin Brockovich*, *Pirates* claims that we should know Bill Gates and Steve Jobs as victims of ambition. The film warrants its "insider" analysis of the causes and effects of the ambitions of its central characters through medium (that is, television)- appropriate spectatorship strategies. These strategies include the film's larger narrative structure that builds upon comparisons and contrasts of key elements of the Steve Jobs and Bill Gates stories; the casting of its main characters and the interviews in the film that these characters offer; and the sense of access to actuality allowed by the alternating indirect and direct address of the interview narration. *Pirates* argues ultimately through its post-modern, ruptured narration of exclusive confessional, that when we allow victims of ambition to become witnesses, ambition itself becomes legible as a cultural value, thriving within and because of flawed, but persisting social systems.

Pirates of Silicon Valley

While *Erin Brockovich* re-creates the knowledge that results from investigation and action, *Pirates* takes for its substance the "insider" view of known events, the respective, interlacing careers of Steve Jobs, co-creator of Apple Computers, and Bill Gates, founder of Microsoft. The film's "inside view" is firmly connected to the known. Within the broad outlines of the careers of its real-life principals, the film anchors its re-creation to actuality by returning to highly public, immediately recognizable images central to its subject, including: Apple's 1984 "Big Brother" Superbowl commercial for the Macintosh; nationally televised sessions announcing collaboration between Apple and Microsoft, featuring Jobs (Noah Wyle) live on stage and Gates (Anthony Michael Hall) "wired" into the event on huge screens on the stage above and behind the podium; and repeated appearances of Jobs and Gates on the covers of national news magazines. These images provide anchors, reference points, that frame the simulated interviews with close, long-time friends and associates of the two main characters. These interviews, most notably with Steve Wozniak (Joey Slotnick) and Steve Ballmer (John Di Maggio), are to offer the close, extended, authoritative disclosures of "what happened" between the key event/images that have made the two careers seem so familiar. The insider interviews function as testimony to what would have been privileged encounters, accessible only to those intimates who would have been there, while offering a means to make the material of the story, its matters of business and technology, immediate and direct because it is personal, rather than distanced. The idea that a movie-of-the-week will tend to dramatize the personal is hardly new. In discussing how these works in general tend to operate on a "human" scale, Gary Edgerton, for example, notes: "The individualized and informal depiction of everyday characters in an assortment of medium shots and close-ups quickly became the forte of the TV movie, moreso than in any other feature film form."[52]   Douglas Gomery concurs, and points out (in his analysis of *Brian's Song* as a prototypical MOW docudrama) that the form works   "by reducing [early 70s racial] issue[s] to the most personal level."[53]   Todd Gitlin suggests that MOWs tell "personal stories an audience will take as revelations of the contemporary."[54]   By drawing on the views of its insiders the drama in *Pirates* becomes not just personal, but more universal, as Martyn Burke, the director of the film explains:

> I became fascinated by the Shakespearean elements in this drama. The betrayal, the scheming, the lust for power, the rise and fall. So that was what I seized on and that was the script that I turned in, and it got a green light almost immediately.[55]

The insider view allowed by the story's central characters emphasizes the truly "Shakespearean" elements present: treachery from without and within, the self-imposed isolation that is particularly problematic for Jobs, and perhaps most important, the size (as well as the rewards and the pitfalls) of the ambitions of both Jobs and Gates. The "inside view" that creates the structure for the film has two key functions in *Pirates*'s larger argument that we gain knowledge through this form of confessional disclosure. The testimony offers basic arguments about the psychology of the main characters. Even more, the various means of re-presenting the insider views, including: cross-cut comparisons at key points in the two sub-narratives; interviews drawing on direct and indirect address, with resulting ruptures of narrative space; and the casting of the film—create strategies of spectatorship that continually emphasize that the hidden and unknown, what has been "inside," now has become visible and accessible. Consequently one of the film's arguments is that we view its very means of re-presentation as a form of public knowledge.

   The people surrounding the central characters in docudramas of ambition qualify how those ambitions can be gratified. *Erin Brockovich* and kindred works such as *A Civil Action, The Hurricane, The Insider*, and even *October Sky* argue that ambition is empowering when put to effective action to help both self and others. The comparable argument in *Pirates* is that ambition is empowering when put to the strategic manipulation of business opponents and co-workers. The effort in *Pirates* to explore the source of ambition sets up its testimonial, "insider" approach. Ironically, the recollections of those closest to Jobs and Gates even from the start only emphasize how isolated, even sociopathic, both are.

The testimony suggests that both men convert multiple desires into their work: conventional desires to succeed and to gain autonomy both compete with and replace a need for personal "success" (Jobs wants the family he never had; Gates wants to control others). By personalizing their stories the film suggests that their work, the development of the microcomputer, was for both men a way to compensate for interpersonal and emotional inadequacies.

Steve Jobs has grand visions for the product his company creates and for the way the company should best be managed. Jobs was a New Age thinker before it was fashionable, envisioning the evolution of Apple and Macintosh computers as an opportunity for individuals to benefit from the synthesis of technology and art. Picasso canvases, a grand piano, and a motorcycle decorate his corporate headquarters as reminders that Apple's corporate philosophy seeks the fusion of art and business. "Real artists ship," he writes on the board during one of his pep talks with his employees. He reminds them repeatedly that "great artists steal." In scene after scene, however, he abuses his employees ("I need artists, not morons, clock-punching losers," he yells at one of his programmers. "Are you a virgin?" he asks one poor "IBM" type mid job interview. "You don't fit in here, why are we wasting our time?")[56] In one scene he encourages a food fight between the Apple and Macintosh development teams. "It's like a family," he says, pleased by the squabbling competition. The issue becomes his adequacy as a father figure. Later, in a company party on the beach, as darkness falls so does civility, and a couple of his employees begin fighting over the need to remain loyal to him. Most of what we see of this part of the story is afforded from the perspective of Steve Wozniak, Jobs's boyhood friend and co-founder of Apple. "Woz" witnesses Jobs's continual rejection of Arlene, his former girl friend. Arlene gives birth to a little girl Jobs vehemently denies is his, even though he names the Lisa, the precursor to the Macintosh, after her. Woz asks on several occasions if it has anything to do with Jobs himself being an adopted child, but never gets a response. Clearly the implication is that Jobs has a problematic family history, and consequently has recreated a dysfunctional family within his own business so that isolation and antagonism can fuel the fires of creativity and productivity.

Gates, on the other hand, becomes isolated by his overwhelming desire to get what he wants at any cost. "I want it!" he shouts, when he sees his first Macintosh. The film characterizes him through his childish and irrepressible impulsiveness, his consistent behavior without regard for consequences. Brief glimpses into his life at Harvard reveal a dorm room chaotically cluttered with bedding, stacks of engineering magazines, plus scattered possessions of the resident who always seems to sleep in his clothes. It provides an appropriate stage for his two passions, playing poker and convincing people that he can build a computer. Later, a motherly secretary rouses Gates from the couch in his office for an appointment. He lives in this space and dresses much as he did as a student. He greets the executive types wearing only crumpled trousers and a T-shirt. In a subsequent scene he is racing through an airport carrying the bundle of dress clothing he's supposed to wear to the critical meeting at IBM, one of the pinnacles of his poker-playing approach to persuasion. Hurriedly dressing in the bathroom, he realizes he has no tie, and so Steve Ballmer, who acts throughout the film as Gates's counterpart to Steve Wozniak, stands on a toilet and haggles the purchase of the necktie of the occupant of the adjacent stall. When Microsoft is a coming company, a photographer preparing to take a publicity photo is appalled at what the CEO is wearing, especially the sweat stains. The difficulty his impulsiveness creates in behaving conventionally carries over to his efforts to engage the opposite sex (he awkwardly bungles his attempt to meet women at a skating party of his own company) and, revealingly, to his driving. He has a Porsche that he likes to drive fast enough, often enough that it lands him in jail. He borrows Paul Allen's new Corvair (Allen, like Ballmer, is another Harvard friend with Gates from the outset). Gates stops at the side of the road where there are two parked bulldozers. He convinces his buddy that not only can they drive the earthmovers, but also that they ought to race them. When he can't stop in time he crushes the side of Allen's car. The scene highlights the key elements of the package: Gates's childishness, his competitiveness, his disregard for rules and laws, and his apparent ability to remain unaffected by the damage caused by his need to have what he wants at any cost.

Their respective ambitions appear to originate from contrasting sources. Jobs needs a squabbling family to fulfill a grand vision of the personal computer as a life style necessity. Gates needs to "win" what he wants no matter what it takes. The ambitions of both men, however, are fueled by facing a common opposition. The repressive, corporate world that they would both plunder tries to ignore or dismiss them. If their work is a form of compensation for personal (and interpersonal) inadequacies, the opponents they face only intensify their desires to succeed through having an impact. Both men would become validated by forced recognition. "For the first time, people are coming to me!" Jobs exclaims to Woz at the Computer Faire that brings the start-up orders for their first computer. In precisely the same moment he manages, ironically and perhaps fatally, to snub Bill Gates and Paul Allen. Gates scams Ed, the Altair company owner who first hires the future Microsoft boys, by claiming that they've received $4000 each for their "other" signing bonuses.

The film's imagery argues that both men begin as marginalized. Jobs as an acid-dropping, ashram-seeking hippie contrasts starkly to Gates as an engineer/nerd who can only fit in with the few friends who surround him. Since they both begin as outsiders they are positioned ideally as contemporary "pirates," ready to raid a corporate world that is repressive in its initial, uncaring disregard, and then to exercise the same kind of disregard when it comes time for them to raid each other.

It is the very blinders the corporate world wears when it comes to the two oddball, fledgling entrepreneurs that invite them to scale the embattlements of capitalism. Early scenes mark the inconsequentiality of both men. Both are forced to come in under the radar of the corporate world. Jobs undergoes a series of humiliating rejections from banks and loan companies as he tries to get seed money so they can fill their first orders. Afraid of creating a harmful first impression, Gates makes Paul Allen pretend to be him when he must go to visit Altair the first time. The conformity both are eventually pushed into—Jobs with his suits and shaved beard, Gates and his ties—indicates the blandness of the corporate envelope both are committed to pushing. The representatives of the corporate world consistently are anonymous, conforming executives wholly lacking in vision. In meeting after meeting, the decision-makers at Hewlitt-Packard, Xerox, and particularly IBM dismiss the significance of the two young wanna-be's and their products.

The conventional, corporate world in *Pirates* is repressive not because of its action, but its inaction, the very blandness and blindness that leads it to ignore the up and coming pirates who push and prod at it until they dominate it. The imagery of Apple's "Big Brother" 1984 Superbowl commercial encapsulates corporate, conventional thinking. The Oz-like talking head dominating the screen on-set depicts established power as immense in its size and control. The vast number of drones the commercial shows as enslaved to this huge, talking head evoke the slaves of Fritz Lang's *Metropolis* (1927), puppets of a fascist regime (who eventually will rise up) but at the outset prove that the controlling power demands and is dependent upon conformity. The climax of the commercial—the woman runner/hammer thrower—suggests that determined, capable individualism can smash through the repressive weight of conventional thinking. The commercial declares war, announcing that ambition will be its key weapon.

In scene after scene Jobs and Gates act on their ambition—become empowered by it—through their ruthless manipulation of associates and opponents. While Jobs continually berates, abuses, and alienates his corporate family, they are shown as a unified group in one notable moment, when they arrive at Xerox to convince the company to let them have the mouse and graphic interface technologies that will be the earmarks of the Macintosh as radical, technological innovation. Gates, on the other hand, often literally depends upon his supporters, for example, as they carry him back to his dorm room and put him to bed, bail him out of jail, roust him out of bed for important appointments, or procure his wardrobe. In projecting his love of poker into his day-to-day interactions, Gates betrays only his opponents: just as he lies to Altair, their first employer, as a way of negotiating higher salaries, he lies to IBM executives in promising them an operating system that he doesn't possess, and of course to Jobs, regarding his intentions toward taking the graphic interface the Macintosh uses and applying it to his own product.

Smaller Screen Spectatorship

Pirates warrants its "insider" analysis of the causes and effects of the ambitions of its central characters through medium (that is, television)-appropriate spectatorship strategies. These strategies include the film's larger narrative structure that builds upon comparisons and contrasts of key elements of the Jobs and Gates stories; the casting of its main characters and the interviews that these characters offer; and the sense of access to actuality allowed by the alternating indirect and direct address of the interview narration.

The "talking heads" of the interviews that comprise the film disclose the personalities of both the speaker and those individuals the speaker talks about. This discussion has tried to show that as the film alternates between stories it parallels both the chronology and the cause/effect linkages of its plot. We are offered comparisons and contrasts of not only the starting points of the ambitions of the main characters ("beating" others with better toys), but also the friendships that translate into co-workers, actions they take against the opposition, and strains in handling the ascent to power. The creation of an interview structure also gives a priority to relationships and their functions.

If interviews are a traditionally appropriate presentational strategy for television, then the casting of the film works strongly in concert with the interview structure to emphasize the narrative's larger arguments about the importance of relationships in this story. The spectatorship strategies of features such as *Changeling* and *Erin Brockovich* center on and grow out of the main character through the interlacing of gazes cast both upon and by its star/character. The comparable strategies in *Pirates* emphasize interaction as the key site of spectatorial focus. Noah Wyle as Steve Jobs and Anthony Michael Hall playing Bill Gates do not come to the work with the aura, the star presence, of a Julia Roberts or an Angelina Jolie. Quite the opposite, in fact: established prior to *Pirates* as ensemble actors (Wyle for his work in *ER*; Hall for his parts in various John Hughes "brat pack" films such as *The Breakfast Club*) the film's casting and the "star" ethos of its respective leads establishes groups and the social contexts their characters will fit within as an appropriate site of spectatorship. If they are group leaders, their best friends and confidantes become the main points of access to those groups. Accordingly Wozniak and Ballmer provide the largest portion of the narration since they are the most "inside" of the insiders.

The interviews provide both direct and indirect address of audience. Indirect address to the unseen interviewer links the material of the interview to long-standing television documentary tradition. The direct address interview mode serves notice that mediation itself plays a key role in the ideas and arguments the film is forwarding. From its opening shot, *Pirates* calls attention to the role of media in its re-creation: Wyle/Jobs is speaking directly to the camera about what Apple is trying to accomplish. The camera arcs around to reveal the second camera shooting the interview, the interviewer, and consequently the mode of address shifts within a few sentences from direct to indirect. As the view widens we see that we are on the set where Ridley Scott's crew is shooting the "Big Brother" commercial. The movement of the camera and the shift in our position as spectators reveals multiple layers of mediation. The film (*Pirates*) we are watching has established an interview being shot regarding a commercial in production that itself, is shown to have another film on the "big" screen, a film that provides the very view of business that will be addressed and modified by the story about to unfold before us.

Direct address foregrounds narrative process, highlighting the advantages and disadvantages, the access and limitations of the narrators' perspectives. The moment when Steve Ballmer explains to us why a meeting of Microsoft and IBM executives had historic importance becomes another moment foregrounding how *Pirates* offers us a superior spectator position. The scene is a logical extension of the film's interview structure and its "insider" view since it takes us most literally "inside" the narrator's perspective. The formal elements of the scene argue collaterally that there really is "no other way to tell it" when it comes to this particularly critical juncture in the fate of the fledgling Microsoft company.

This begins as one of a number of conference scenes, set up by the rush to catch the plane and to provide Gates with the tie that will allow a fitting wardrobe for the meeting. The parties seated around the table discuss the kind of business that they can do, and Gates (as he does throughout the film) tells the opposition that Microsoft can provide what they truly need. In this case it will be a disk operating system for microcomputers, a system that they don't own and haven't invented. Thus the idea for DOS is sold to IBM at the moment of inception.

As Gates makes this offer, the action of the scene freezes. The camera pulls back to put the conference table in the background, and leaves Ballmer in the foreground. Ballmer turns to us, "steps out" of the conference room shot and begins to talk directly to the camera, pointing out how this moment is a turning point, truly the beginning of the Microsoft fortune. The conference remains framed, as though in an historical painting. As a privileged insider, through the formal strategies of his narration, specifically the rupture of conventional narrative space created by the control over narrative process the interview exerts, he has taken us even further "inside" his story to lay bare his perspective, allowing us to share through his perceptions the privilege of his position. The freezing of all movement save his own, the movement to the "outside" of the time of the scene so that its witness may comment to us upon it asserts a further movement to the "inside" of events, allowing us to glimpse the "truth" of what could not otherwise be shown, and also allowing to see, with emphatic clarity, the nature of the material presenting that knowledge.

A number of reviewers of *Pirates* commented on the "ironic," "mocking" tone of the film.[57] The film's intertextuality—its systematic references to key, "known" images and events, and its self-referential re-presentation of its own means of disclosure—allow *Pirates* to argue that docudramatic mediation offers an appropriate form of knowledge, particularly when strategies of spectatorship are integral to its subject matter.

Knowing What We See

A basic function of docudrama is to make visible the known but unseen, to bring to light the hidden, the otherwise inaccessible. *Erin Brockovich, Changeling, A Mighty Heart,* and a number of comparable pre-2000 feature film biopics and events docudramas (*The Hurricane, The Insider, A Civil Action, Ghosts of Mississippi, Donnie Brasco,* and *Amistad,* for example) accomplish this purpose by asserting that investigation offers knowledge, and to re-create the action of investigation allows the opportunity to make that knowledge public. As feature films, their focus on action and its consequences, coupled with star casting (Jolie; Roberts; Washington; Crowe; Travolta) and large-screen presentation gives their stories the most literal kind of size and scope.

By contrast, a movie-of-the-week such as *The Pirates of Silicon Valley* (or *The Positively True Adventures of the Texas Cheerleader Murdering Mom* [M. Ritchie, 1993]; or *Shannon Mohr: A Victim of Love* [J. Cosgrove, 1993]) asserts that public knowledge can result from re-creating disclosure, the testimony or confessions of real-life principals who have had direct, authoritative access to the actuality they discuss. The "dialogue" they open with us is not only appropriate to the means of presentation, but it also draws on its strengths, its abilities to select material, show it, and then also discuss it directly. Different media necessitate different strategies of mediation, however both feature film and movie-of-the-week docudramas share the premise that their means of re-presentation offer argument, and that those arguments, in part, offer their spectators varying forms of knowledge. Janet Staiger has taken up the issue of how texts responding to each other references the real. She notes that:

> The intertextuality I have in mind is not simply a moment in a text or some relation between two texts, but rather a fundamental and unceasing spectatorial activity, the semiotic action of processing a filmic narrative by repeated referencing and referring to other texts. Intertextuality as understood from a poststructuralist perspective is a constant and irretrievable circulation of textuality, a returning to, a pointing toward, an aggressive attempt to seize other documents. The results of this procedure of referencing other texts are also complicity and irrevocably circular and ideological.[58]

In her discussion of the re-presentation of testimony in *The Return of Martin Guere* Staiger adds: "Even if one could say that the film in some sense really did represent completely the physical or visible world of the

1500s, it would be said within an ideology that what is visible is what is real."[59]   Consequently what is excessively visible—for example, the moment of witnessing an event—warrants its claims to the real through the clear ideological markers that identify and define discourse as testimony.   In the cases of features such as *Erin Brockovich* and MOWs like *Pirates*, both kinds of works draw upon the ideology of the "visible" to position us, as spectators, to believe that to the extent that we can know anything we "know" what we see.   The re-creation that characterizes feature film and movie-of-the-week docudrama necessarily generates intertextuality.   Accordingly, these works argue in part that forms of spectatorship become forms of public knowledge, or more specifically, a kind of knowledge based on, and circumscribed by strategies of re-presentation.

We are offered different views on how ambition can be both destructive and empowering when put to effective action. *Erin Brockovich* shows that by taking the publicly known (the fact of the settlement reached with PG&E and its size) and telling the story as a feature film, the docudrama both warrants its view of its subject and forwards that argument in a way appropriate to the medium of presentation. By comparison, as a movie-of-the-week *Pirates* offers a similar opportunity to examine the interrelationship of means of re-presentation, choice of subject, argument(s) that result, and the spectatorship strategies that forward those arguments.

Despite the striking differences in their respective styles of re-presentation, both works ultimately confirm the view they share that ambition can thrive within flawed, but persisting social systems. In doing so both films end with a wink at their viewer.   Erin receives her commission check, but the final image of the film shows her knocking on "our" door, staring directly into the camera at us, suggesting the continuation of the scope of her energy, the need for her work, and her commitment to it. The epilogue of *Pirates* reiterates the well-known fates of its principals, reconfirming the costs as well as the benefits of the ambitions it has disclosed. Both works argue, ultimately, for the necessity of allowing victims to become witnesses so that their testimony can enter public knowledge and public memory, whether it is through *EB*'s classic suturing of the actions of victimization, exposure, and public event, or *Pirates*'s post-modern, ruptured narration of exclusive confessional.

CHAPTER SIX

THE EVENTS ARENA REVISITS THE WEST, OR: HORSES, WORK AND THE *SEABISCUIT* SYNDROME: CAN EQUINE EXEMPLARS KEEP US ON TRACK?

In late 2003 and early 2004, Hollywood released two docudramas about horses that reached substantial audiences. *Seabiscuit* (G. Ross, 2003) adapted the successful nonfiction account by Laura Hillenbrand of the famous racehorse and his owner, trainer, and jockey. *Hidalgo* (J. Johnston, 2004) was "based on the life of Frank T. Hopkins" and extracted from a number of Hopkins's stories of his life as a late nineteenth century cowboy, stories containing claims that subsequently have been challenged as to their truth and authenticity.[60] Clearly, the time was right for "true stories" about horses, but why? It comes as no surprise that Disney studios produced *Hidalgo* because it wanted a film to compete directly with *Seabiscuit*. This race to release films about horse racing suggests the studios saw 2003 as a ripe time to give audiences this kind of story. At this point in American history—two years after 9/11, months after the invasion of Iraq, and as the culture wars that characterized the 2004 presidential race were heating up—the push to get out these two productions suggests both films revisit, recover, and reinforce—rescue—a traditional vision of American identity precisely at the most problematic of times. Both films rework for a contemporary audience the mythology of effort integral to a mid-twentieth century, immigrant-rooted American culture's traditional sense of "success," arguing that who we are as Americans is best defined as unfettered will in action. Horses become a means in both films to argue that through will, work, and effort we have the capacity to overcome fundamental social flaws, including class differences (in *Seabiscuit*) and ethnic prejudice (in *Hidalgo*). The films contribute to this traditional mythology of effort as a cornerstone of American success through two basic, shared strategies. First, the films revisit the iconography of horses as emblems of American culture.

Seabiscuit adds to its "revisioning" of horses the relatable imagery of Depression nostalgia. Second, but in different ways, both films emphasize that the process of mythologizing American identity and self-worth is itself a process of storytelling. Both films, as docudramas, in taking on the task of dramatizing documents, tell us stories about storytelling. While *Hidalgo* adapts and embraces its teller's own mythology, *Seabiscuit* re-creates as a successive process of storytelling the means by which audiences were invited to identify with the legendary race horse, his effort, his power, his legendary "kick" in the back stretch, and the hope created by efforts against the odds.

Revisiting the West

The releases not only of *Seabiscuit* and *Hidalgo*, but also at almost the same time *Open Range* (2003) and *Cold Mountain* (2003) suggest that the iconography of horses, as well as that of the frontier itself as three of the films in this group revisit it, become once again useful discursive arenas within which to argue for a vision of contemporary self-definition. Despite their substantial differences in plot, character, and setting, all four of these films center on how place and relationships affect personal identity: *Cold Mountain*'s main character becomes a heroine in adapting to her new home in the wilderness as she consummates her relationship with her lover; *Open Range*'s hero finds his status and his true love in defending his right to move his herd through disputed land; Frank, Hidalgo's rider, finds himself when he and his equine partner shift what they do to another continent; and Seabiscuit and his support group must prove themselves throughout—and to—the entire U.S. As stories of exemplification, all four films explore what it takes to become better people, and consequently moral systems drive their narrative structures. It is in *Hidalgo* and *Seabiscuit* in particular, however, that horses provide the link between identity and morality, placing horses at the centers of the moral systems of their respective films. In both, horses become the reference points for moral values and moral behavior, and these clearer value systems are essential for finding the true self worth that both films argue defines personal identity.

Horses and the Iconography of the Western

Not surprisingly, horses are so much a part of the settings that frame the traditional iconography of the western that we tend to accept unquestioningly their presence and their contributions. Horses are integral to the setting of the west, and Will Wright argues that it is the elements of setting that provide the foundation for the morality that westerns explore:

> In the mythical context, it is clear how the land that embodies such meanings can become a fount of social values. Individuality, respect, acceptance, strength, freedom, and goodness are all associated with and therefore derived from the mountains and the deserts, lakes and streams of the west. The Western myth has taken the historical setting and shaped it into a model of the present, which states in concrete images the conceptual conflicts of modern America and resolves them through types of action.[61]

As an element of this setting and the moral systems it conveys, horses have fulfilled several functions: they are (like other aspects of nature) a resource to be exploited; they offer heroic service; they allow the extension of human will; and as such, horses become an element of character and cultural identity in westerns.

Horses are linked inextricably with our sense of identity as Americans. America has been called "the greatest horse country in the world"[62] in part because horses from England, Holland, Spain, and elsewhere arrived with the European immigration to, occupation, exploration, and exploitation of the lands that become America.

As such, because they are "tamed" beasts horses embody the blending of nature and culture that in the western film, positions the natural world as a potentially exploitable resource. Hidalgo and Seabiscuit serve to remind us what past, more horse-dependent American cultures have lived: horses not only are emblematic of diversity, but also are indexes of worth and responsibility. The importance of horses begins with their use potential, the service they can render. In western films, horses allow mobility, enabling human characters to act and so to fulfill their mythic functions on the sides of justice and injustice, weakness and strength, and good and evil.[63] As a means of facilitating human movement, horses function as media in the literal sense that Marshall McLuhan had in mind when he defined any medium as a means of extending the human body.[64] Horses facilitate reach, mobility, and consequently (for better or worse) become a means of actualizing human will.

The selflessness with which they do so places horses squarely on the side of good in the western film scheme of values, where evil begins with the selfish exploitation of natural resources (first and most lethally prosecutable on the list in any western naturally being horse-stealing, followed by cattle-rustling, then land-grabbing, mineral-grabbing, etc.).[65] The unhesitating service and companionship horses provide allows them to become easily anthropomorphosized as loyal servants, steadfast companions, and partners.[66] Ultimately through their selflessness, their feats of great strength and endurance, and their superhuman accomplishments, horses become heroic, imbued with the best and most useful of human values. Like the "frontier" itself, horses function charismatically in contemporary narrative discourse: they signify what we need them to. Our very language indicates the extent to which we compare what horses mean to our sense of self worth and human values, ranging from groundedness (having horse sense) to pretentiousness (being on a high horse) to blatant foolishness (when horsing around leads one ultimately to becoming a complete horse's ass).[67]

Horses have contributed to the formation of American culture and American character in endeavors of work, war, and amusement. The strength and speed we associate with horses arguably are to a large extent responsible for the great importance American culture places on winning, and particularly relevant here, a fascination with racing.

Seabiscuit and Public Memory

Seabiscuit's feature-length adaptation of Hillenbrand's book focuses the meaning of winning on the horse's rivalry with War Admiral. The building confrontation between Seabiscuit and War Admiral sets up a series of cultural oppositions: Samuel Riddle (Eddie Jones), War Admiral's owner, belittles the challenge from Charles Howard (Jeff Bridges) and team Seabiscuit because he sees them as western commoners undeserving of the same consideration as eastern aristocracy. Newsreels reinforce the image. They proclaim War Admiral's "perfection" in size, speed, and records in running in the great, established races on the Eastern seaboard. Seabiscuit's larger challenge is to disprove the equation between class, background, and inherent worth.

Seabiscuit's victory over War Admiral ultimately becomes a victory for a view of democratic culture. It proves nurtured ability and self-belief as the equalizers in the larger argument for the validity of individual effort. The film argues that most fundamentally, the power of the horse is that it extends human potential. The relationships that result between horses and individuals complete and restore the family as a source of support, and conversely, the family empowers those within it. "Horsepower" here becomes empowerment, and an argument for hope. The case of Seabiscuit reinforces the most traditional, mythic value of individual effort as the key to overcoming obstacles and succeeding in American society. In order to show how "Seabiscuit" becomes a cultural signifier, however, *Seabiscuit* functions docudramatically, adapting a story about a real-life legend as a story about storytelling. Storytelling becomes integral to the process of empowerment, providing the bridge from individual effort and accomplishment to social inspiration, the larger cultural function of the story. *Seabiscuit* argues that storytelling as well is a response to "horse power." Storytelling offers a means to extend experiencing the benefits of the power of horses outward to others, to society generally. Storytelling structures the processes of identification, participation, and inspiration, linking identity and hope. The storytelling dimensions of the Seabiscuit story, fundamental to the functions of settings in this events docudrama, show not only how Seabiscuit became cultural property, but also operate as actuality anchors, warranting the claims the film forwards about what is exemplary in this instance.

Seabiscuit develops the storyteller roles of Charles Howard, the horse's owner, Red Pollard (Tobey Maguire), Seabiscuit's jockey, and emphasizes the invented role of Tick Tock McLaughlin (William H. Macy), a radio commentator on the racing scene, who becomes an effective press agent for Seabiscuit's rising career. The film also incorporates historical storytelling strategies into its narrative structure and mise en scene, allowing documentary material to frame its story. The interaction of historical material and narrative re-creation foregrounds storytelling as an element of the Seabiscuit phenomenon, and warrants the assertions the film is making about the importance of the story. The film's emphasis on storytelling clarifies the importance of Seabiscuit as cultural property. We see the progressive steps in the public relations process that shift the horse into public ownership, and how those steps framed public perceptions of horse, rider, trainer, and owner as underdogs, commoners who have only their innate abilities and their willingness to try.

One of the main ways that *Seabiscuit* is a story about storytelling is that three of its main characters are storytellers. Storytelling is integral to Red. It created the culture of his biological family and formed his character as an adult. The quotation from Emily Dickinson we see the young Red struggling to complete around the dinner table, furthermore, foreshadows the kind of literature of inspiration that the Seabiscuit story would become ("We never know how high we are ...").[68] Red is constantly associated with his books, constantly reading when he is not riding, and we see Red's identity articulated through literature at several points in the story: while a struggling jockey he tells locker room tales of the epic races he's won in far off lands; he throws Shakespeare while on horseback to reporters eager for a quote ("Tho he be but little, he is fierce" [*A Midsummer Night's Dream*, Act III, Sc. 2]); he quotes Hadrian to Seabiscuit while they are recovering from their injuries ("Brick by brick, my citizens"); and thrusts Shakespeare again (*Julius Caesar*; Act III, Sc. 2) at the Howards and Tom when he feels they've betrayed him by not allowing him to ride Seabiscuit after he's been instrumental in healing the horse ("This, the cruelest cut of all"). Most ironically, his injury forces Red to be on the receiving end of a story, a news broadcast, to follow Seabiscuit's victory in his definitive race against War Admiral. Red relates to and is related to the world through stories.

In a similar way Charles Howard's function as horse owner shifts him into the role of storyteller. Charles is constantly presenting himself, his intentions, and his own sense of hope as story. Early on Charles integrates public relations work into his entrepreneurship. He explains the role of motorcars and racecars to customers and crowds as the destiny of society ("the future is the finish line"). He repeats this same line after Seabiscuit's first win, and subsequently in his Capra-esque framing of the small race horse as a David taking on the Goliaths of the racing world ("This is a horse with a lot of heart ... He didn't let it get to him ... He doesn't know he's little, he thinks he's the biggest horse out here ... when a little guy, who doesn't know he's a little guy, he can do great big things ... The future is the finish line, and the 'Biscuit is just the horse to get us there.") Later, in riling up public pressure on Riddle and War Admiral, he tells an eager crowd at a rail stop, "The horse is too small, the jockey too big, the trainer too old, and I'm too dumb to know the difference!" In a scene that resembles a political stump speech, he tells a crowd at another stop, standing on the back of the last car on the train, the "Seabiscuit Special," "You're here to see him because this is a horse that won't give up." Howard's PR work makes Seabiscuit relatable to the largest public possible, drawing on the ideals of possibility, self-made opportunity, and self belief.

To supplement and extend Howard's public relations efforts, Tick Tock McLaughlin, who broadcasts a regular radio commentary on the racing scene, cues, leads, and shapes public perception of Seabiscuit. Recurring scenes of Tick Tock in his home-made studio feature a couch, a female collaborator who always looks slightly put upon, and a motley collection of sound effects devices that would make a Foley artist proud. Tick Tock's broadcasts characterize his work as a creative process, emphasizing the constructed nature of shaping the Seabiscuit story and the importance of broadcasting that story to an increasing (and increasingly enthusiastic) audience. Tick Tock fuels the momentum in the PR war that leads the run-up to the confrontation with War Admiral by calling attention not only to the horse's record, but the bandwagon effect his performances generate. Seabiscuit begins as the "skunk in the garden party" when he is first raced, but quickly McLaughlin is saying that "he made a believer out of me" and pointing out that the horse is "selling out the cheap seats." His repeated comments on the crowds that pack the tracks correlate the "common man" audience and attention with the immensity of the victory, confirming indirectly the effectiveness of the campaign to complete Seabiscuit as story, making the horse the property of the largest possible audience and elevating his accomplishments to the status of cultural phenomenon. The addition of McLaughlin's character as a storytelling device, much like the film itself, reminds us how "Seabiscuit" entered (and now re-enters) public memory through the portal of storytelling.

Given the film's strategies to re-create Seabiscuit as an element of the culture of democratic myth during the Depression years, it is not surprising that the film foregrounds its own strategies for incorporating historical material into its narrative fabric. *Seabiscuit* begins with a montage of vintage photographs of cars and American city life at the turn of the twentieth century. Recalling the work he did on *The Civil War* and *Baseball*, David Mcullough's voice-over comments on the impact of the automobile on American society, tying the mixed blessing of individual mobility to historical and cultural change. The film's own Ken Burns-like interweaving of voice-over commentary and primary documentary material—photographs, broadcasts, and newspapers—anchors the story in American history generally, but also more specifically focuses on the building confrontation between Seabiscuit and War Admiral as a bona fide cultural event. The voice-over allows a flexible, filtered perspective that provides the authority of overall knowledge (Mccullough's status as historian) on a personal scale. The narrator's simple, direct statements make the larger historical context immediate. On industrialization and the age of the automobile: "It was the beginning and end of imagination, all at the same time." On Prohibition: "At a time when you really needed a drink, you couldn't get one." On the New Deal as relief: "For the first time in a long time, some one cared; we were no longer alone."[69] Through the overall strategy of history as story, made personal by the comfort of a storyteller's voice and rhetoric, the forces evident in Seabiscuit's challenge to the racing world (as an unknown, disadvantaged outsider and commoner) appear as elements of conflict in a story. The battle between Seabiscuit and War Admiral becomes framed through storytelling processes as a cultural event. We first see Riddle, War Admiral's owner, in news stories, then responding to the challenge of Seabiscuit in newsreel clips of his own press conferences. His comments convey class snobbery. "You wouldn't put Dempsey in the ring with a middle weight." He calls

War Admiral "a superior horse with superior breeding … it won't make any difference who [Seabiscuit's] passenger is." As the "Seabiscuit Special" moves east an old-fashioned montage of spinning headlines and switchboard calls shows the mounting public enthusiasm for the confrontation. The race itself begins not with shots of the track, the riders, the horses, or the stands, but photographs of people anywhere but the track, listening to radios in their homes and cars. Over this we hear the radio broadcast of the track announcer's voice, before shifting to the race itself. As an event that is "momentous" because it has been framed for the public, *Seabiscuit* makes the logical move of re-creating the "moment" of the race as the media covered it. The film presents the moment it has built to, the beginning of the Seabiscuit-War Admiral race itself, as a collage of self-narrating, primary historical material.

Seabiscuit re-creates this epic confrontation between legendary race horses as an event with wide-spread public participation. By becoming the audience for the Seabiscuit story the on-screen audience as well as the audience for the film itself complete the storytelling process. Sharing through participation in the story, the film argues, becomes empowering, for the principal figures who function as storytellers, for the public they told their stories to, as well as for us, now. Through the Seabiscuit story, we return to and participate once more in the mythic functions of the American horse. Horses, like storytelling itself, allow mobility, the opportunity to extend our will, and in so doing reinforce our sense of ourselves. Seabiscuit is exemplary because his story argues that your efforts will bear fruit if you believe in yourself. Stories are a means to create and sustain that belief. One's sense of self, the film argues, begins with this effort, especially when effort becomes hardest, when it is born of the loss of those reference points we rely upon for self definition, such as family and work. The example of Seabiscuit and Seabiscuit's reassertion of that example in public memory puts that necessary self-belief and the effort that results into the context of a culture that, the story claims, rewards effort that perseveres despite the obstacles that confront it. If we can relate to Seabiscuit, then we can understand that who we are is not determined by what others think of us, but by the quality of what we do. Ultimately, *Seabiscuit* reasserts the near limitless exploitability of what horses offer, reaffirming one of the cornerstones of American culture, the sense we crave that we can always go back to the well and draw a little more.

CHAPTER SEVEN

SOUNDING OUT THE RIGHT:
CLARENCE THOMAS, ANITA HILL,
AND CONSTRUCTING SPIN
IN THE NAME OF JUSTICE

The polarization that has characterized American politics so sharply since the 1980s appears to worsen with each election cycle. The divisiveness of the political arena indicates the codes and constraints that create contestation when key players seek to translate personal ambition into public practice. The docudramas set in the political arena that I will consider here and in the next chapters illuminate the intersection of private tensions, the constraints of political processes, and the resulting impact on public knowledge and public memory.

The made-for-television docudrama *Strange Justice* (E. Dickerson, 1999) revisits the events during the tempestuous summer of 1991 that saw the ascendance of Clarence Thomas to the United States Supreme Court. The film shows us how and why Anita Hill stepped forward to oppose the nomination, and the response to the confrontation by the United States Senate Judiciary Committee. The film bases much of its re-creation on transcripts of press conferences and Judiciary Committee hearings. Through its weaving together of actual and re-created sound and image materials, the film's suturing strategies both model and deconstruct the "spin" that framed Thomas's campaign for confirmation and Hill's opposition. *Strange Justice* is an analysis of spin, as its own suturing of real and re-created materials models the very processes it exposes of shaping public perception, opinion, and memory. The exposure of where and how the real and the fabricated interact reveals how Thomas became an effective construction of the political right, forecasting how those same strategies would be brought into play in present-day politics of presidential power and Supreme Court nominations.

"Spin" has become an everyday term, describing the process of using the media to frame people, actions, and events in order to shape public perception and ultimately public opinion. We understand that spin entails a blend of the real and its construction, a strategic mixture of fact and myth. The work of "spin," or, if you will, spinning "the real" has two literal senses that show the appropriateness of the term: To "spin" something means to turn it, so that we can view it and perhaps see it differently from multiple perspectives, while "spinning" also suggests the manufacturing of thread, from which the spinner can weave cloth. These literal and figurative meanings of "spin" all apply in the case of *Strange Justice*.

The Showtime Networks aired *Strange Justice* in September of 1999, fully eight years after the events occurred that this "based on a true story" work re-recreates.[70] As a movie-of-the-week docudrama, *Strange Justice* frames real and re-created events within the overall form of a classic Hollywood narrative. The "true story" we see in this case balances well-known, widely-seen documentary imagery with events that did not occur before network television cameras. Consequently *Strange Justice* covers the announcement of Thomas's nomination to the Court, the preparation for his nomination hearings, the subsequent U.S. Senate Judiciary Committee confirmation hearings, including the key testimony by both Thomas and Anita Hill, and the repercussions Hill's charges created. *Strange Justice* approaches this basic subject matter as a combination of history and political psychodrama. At key moments during hearings the work shifts between straightforward documentary material, conventional narrative re-creation of events and the principals involved, and highly theatricalized interpretation of the testimony. The perspective the film offers is to view these events through the prism of docudrama, and specifically as a true story about storytelling. The overall argument *Strange Justice* develops is that the legal, political, and ethical issues raised by the Thomas nomination should be understood most fruitfully as the product of initiating and reformulating Thomas's story. Within this larger approach the film then shows us the "whole cloth" spun from this process by foregrounding the blend of actuality and re-creation in specific scenes and sequences.

There are several reasons why the Clarence Thomas nomination story is best understood as a matter of spin. First, the Thomas nomination provides a glaring and consequently illustrative instance of how effectively over several decades conservative political interests in the United States have marshaled the means to manipulate public opinion. Second, Thomas himself, as the embodiment of paradoxes of race and identity, invited the possibility of being perceived from multiple perspectives. Third, as Thomas's nomination hearing became a forum for the exercise of power by conservative political interests the process redefined the public perception of the roles of victimizer and victim. This abuse of process culminated in Thomas's confirmation, as well as allowing conservative committee members the opportunity to serve as advocates on Thomas's behalf, rather than functioning as impartial servants of the larger public interest.

Spin By the Masters

To review: following on the heels of embedded journalists, the exploitation of Jessica Lynch, the deflection of responsibility for Abu Ghraib, the performances of Condoleeza Rice and Donald Rumsfeld before the 9/11 Commission, and the various and sundry fictions of the 2004 U. S. presidential campaign ("town hall" meetings; Swiftboat Veterans for Truth), early 2005 saw some (belated) attention turned to the George W. Bush administration's efforts to control the media, in, for example, its support of a fake White House press correspondent, its investment of substantial amounts of taxpayer dollars to pay former journalist Karen Ryan to produce government public relations pieces, to pay columnist Armstrong Williams $240,000 to promote No Child Left Behind, to stage "conversations" on its proposed reform of Social Security, to create a Department of Homeland Security public relations campaign, and to produce and distribute on evening newscasts video "news" releases.[71] Conservative political interests in the U.S., however, systematically have developed financial and organizational resources in order to spin their stories since briefly losing the White House to Jimmy Carter. The Clarence Thomas nomination was supported and promoted by conservative foundations begun in the 1970s (most notably the Heritage Foundation and its offshoot, the Free Congress Foundation).[72] The likelihood that a Thomas nomination would aid the causes of re-institutionalizing prayer in public schools, the overturn of Roe v. Wade, and the curtailment of gay rights earned it support from the alliance of black and white religious conservative groups that had become prominent during the Reagan administration, including Jerry Falwell's Moral Majority, and the Citizens Committee, an organization of white evangelical ministers.[73] In sum, the Thomas nomination fit neatly into a twenty-year sustained effort by conservative interests to "form strategic alliances around common issues they support" and had developed the resources to promote.[74]

As a conservative African American, Thomas-as-nominee offered a veritable rainbow of opportunities for spin. During the Reagan administration

Supreme Court nominations became a focal point for the consolidation of conservative, if not right-wing political power. As of early 2005, seven out of nine sitting Supreme Court justices had been appointed by Republican presidents (Stevens by Ford; O'Connor, Rehnquist, Scalia, and Kennedy by Reagan; Souter and Thomas by the first President Bush). The nomination of Robert Bork in 1987 failed in part because the NAACP opposed his record on civil rights, thus the pragmatic, strategic advantage to a Republican administration of the Thomas nomination.[75]

Thomas's record as head of the Equal Employment Opportunity Commission (EEOC) during the Reagan administration and his subsequent appointment to the D.C. Circuit Court posed some basic paradoxes that necessitated spinning the candidate to ensure his confirmation. Thomas had taken public stances against Affirmative Action, even though he had benefited from it in his admissions to Holy Cross and Yale, yet his job as the head of EEOC was to enforce its provisions.[76] Thomas felt that Affirmative Action stigmatized its beneficiaries, creating what he called "black work," yet in his first appearances before the public and the Senate Judiciary Committee he embraced the mythology of growing up poor and black in Pinpoint, Georgia. Thomas was nominated to the Supreme Court even though he "had never litigated a case before a jury" … "nor, during his brief stint as a judge, had he issued a single substantive constitutional opinion"[77]—a record due in part perhaps because he had joined a D.C. Circuit bench that had featured the likes of Robert Bork, Antonin Scalia, and Ken Starr.[78]

Given the multiple perspectives Thomas's record as a nominee allowed, and the commitment the conservative core of the Republican party had made to ensuring his nomination, it is no surprise that the public's perception of Thomas required its most extreme molding during the Senate nomination hearings as Anita Hill's claims finally became public that she had been sexually harassed by Thomas when they both worked at the EEOC. In essence, Hill's charges and the Committee's efforts to deflect them made strikingly evident how the Senate Judiciary Committee's process had been focused on its construction of Thomas. Sticking to this story highlighted the identity politics grounding the redefinition of the roles of all involved. Analyses by Jane Flax, Toni Morrison, and Hill herself[79] have examined in detail the ways rhetorical elements of the Thomas hearings display how bald the exercise of the politics of race and identity became at this moment. I would like to draw upon this larger discussion to focus briefly on how *Strange Justice* depicts the role changes the work of spin created. Specifically Thomas, with the encouragement of the Committee, recast himself as victim and Hill as victimizer, and the Committee, departing from its role as evaluators, became collaborators with Thomas in this construction project, and then became his advocates.

In the first (and what originally was to be the only) round of hearings, Thomas embraced the confirmation process as the culmination of the opportunity America had offered him. The second set of hearings allowed Hill to testify and Thomas to rebut. Jane Flax and others have argued that the commitment the Committee had made to Thomas prevented it from entertaining the recognition of Thomas as victimizer and Anita Hill as a victim; in fact, the case is just the opposite.[80] Hill's testimony threatened the shared "American Dream" narrative that Thomas and the Committee in concert had fashioned, and consequently made it necessary for the process to expunge Hill.[81] Here with the help of the Committee Thomas changes his role from one offered fulfillment through his participation in a Horatio Alger-like American upward mobilization, to, ironically, one who has been damaged by the very same process. In calling the Committee's airing of Hill's charges "a high tech lynching for uppity blacks" in one of its most notorious moments Thomas suggests he has been victimized both by the confirmation process itself, and by an irrational, duplicitous African American woman's exploitation of his sexual and racial identity.[82]

Strange Justice and Spin

In re-creating the evolution of this role reversal *Strange Justice* illuminates the dynamics of how the culmination of Thomas's nomination before the Senate Judiciary Committee invited a confirmation hearing to serve an explicitly political process. This is evident in the film's larger structure, as well as in specific scenes that re-create the hearings themselves. While a number of the film's critics noted the "edgy" and even "surreal" elements of the hearing scenes, I would like to focus more on how, in these moments, the film equates political power with acoustic space in its adaptation of the video transcript of the hearing.

Strange Justice argues most fundamentally that the best storyteller gains and maintains political power. Consequently the structure of the film models the processes it tells about and ultimately re-creates. This is evident in both character and plot. The film depicts the main players in Thomas's camp as engaged in constructing the Thomas story, often in conflict with each other as to the best way to let the story be told. Central to this is Ken Duberstein (Mandy Patinkin), the handler hired by the Republican party to manage the Thomas nomination. Thomas himself (Delroy Lindo) comes to oppose Duberstein's recommendations and strategies for what Thomas should say, and how he should say it. The film shows one of the most remembered moments of the 1991 trial[83] as this conflict between narratives reaching a climax when Thomas rejects Duberstein's recommended response to Anita Hill's testimony and creates one of his own that depicts him as victim of lynching. Subordinates work to facilitate the agendas of these sometimes aligned, sometimes conflicting narrators. The film's re-creation of the equation of storytelling and power places Anita Hill (Regina Taylor) in the position of offering a single story, a sole voice that can't compete with the voices that rise up to oppose it. The Senate Judiciary committee minimizes or denies the opportunities to hear the stories of witnesses who would support Hill. We see the system redefine Hill's role from speaker to listener, from witness with testimony to listener denied a venue for an adequate response.

In addition to its depiction of characters as storytellers, *Strange Justice* also frames the history of the nomination as a process of spinning the Thomas story by converting chronology itself into story structure. The film's narrative arc breaks down into three stages the events transpiring during the two months from the announcement of Thomas's nomination to his swearing in ceremony. The first, expository stage explains the political purpose underlying the nomination; as one aide comments, the Bush administration is "going to really stick it to the liberals on this one." The "stick" is that as an African American, ultra-conservative judge with a track record antagonistic toward the rights of women and minorities Clarence Thomas embodies ideological paradoxes. Larger narrative conflicts unfold and intensify in the second stage of this structure when preparations for framing Thomas's story in the upcoming confirmation hearings encounter opposing stories: Thomas's religious propriety becomes countered by allegations of spousal abuse and ultimately challenged most severely when the Anita Hill story comes to light.

The culmination of initiating and framing the Thomas story requires, in the last stage of events, the recasting of Thomas as a victim of the ideologues of the left. Here the on-screen storytelling processes most explicitly seize the power of definition, defining Thomas as an innocent in need of rescue, and Hill, his antagonist, as a liar, a dupe, and a plagiarist, whose sanity is questionable.

Strange Justice is both narration and demonstration. Within the story it tells about how conservative interests packaged and sold Clarence Thomas, the film illuminates its own docudramatic storytelling processes. Just as "spin" is a framing of an actuality to create perception and define its meaning, scenes throughout *Strange Justice* bring together real and re-created sounds and images to interact.[84] For example, during the initial press conference announcing Thomas's nomination, the re-created Clarence Thomas appears to stand next to the actual George Bush. I'll discuss momentarily how *Strange Justice*'s presentation of the Senate confirmation hearing cuts between its video transcript of the Judiciary Committee and the reverse angles of the reactions of Thomas and Anita Hill. The juxtaposition within the same cinematic space legitimizes the view of events the film presents, bolstering the basis in truth the "based on a true story" narrative claims.

To illustrate *Strange Justice*'s own spinning of the real I'd like to focus on a key moment when the film presents one of its central arguments, that telling the Thomas story successfully demanded seizing the power of role definition, effectively reversing the perception of victimizer and victim. "The *Exorcist*" portion of the Thomas confirmation hearings in *Strange Justice* exemplifies the film's analysis of the process of spin. The bedrock of this scene is its sound, the transcript of the actual hearing. *Strange Justice* allows the public record, the documentary material, to interact in several ways with what was not documented but can only be reported or inferred. In this instance testimony and response to it set up the interplay of public and private space. Specifically we see the actuality in the public record of committee action to define Anita Hill's role, and the re-creation of her response.

In the "*Exorcist*" scene we see Thomas's supporters, with Orrin Hatch as their spokesman, riding to the rescue of their nominee. The scene sutures documentary material and re-creation, public and private space, to foreground Hatch's dual role as advocate as well as accuser. Hatch here is presenting testimony and evidence on Thomas's behalf in order to reframe the committee's and the public's perception of Hill. As the scene evolves Hatch's accusations define Hill as a dupe of the left, a plagiarist, and ultimately as irrational for putting her accusations before the public. The interplay consequently positions Hill as accused, with no commensurate forum available for recourse or response. Thomas, the object of all this, remains a bystander while Hatch takes the lead.

The construction of the scene sets several kinds of docudramatic interactions in motion to carry out the progressive accusations and framing of Hill. The videotaped transcript of the hearing, its sound in particular, give the scene its spine, providing two-thirds of its framework. Brief cut-aways from documentary to re-created material show Thomas's affirmation of Hatch's points, and the responses of Hill and her supporters while they watch the hearings in her hotel room. Beyond simply setting up the interplay of public space that is "on the record" and the re-created representation of reaction to it, the juxtapositions and the interactions that

result illuminate the exercise of power at this moment. Hatch's presentation
and the procedure of the committee are real and present before the public.
As he acts as Thomas's advocate Hatch gives the support Thomas has in
the Senate from like-minded conservatives actuality, weight, and
momentum. The scene shows both Thomas and Hill for what they are in
the process, quite literally, constructions of the discourse that has put them
on the public agenda.

The presentation Hatch is making appears to follow a kind of cause-
effect logic: the "digging up the dirt" by the left that Thomas has alluded
to in prior testimony leads to unearthing the likely source of the infamous
"pubic hair on the Coke" claim, in *The Exorcist*. That Hill would testify to
this shows her as a pawn of the left, a plagiarist (Hatch says, "I submit,
those things were found"), possibly irrational ("she would have us believe
that you were saying these things because you wanted to date her?") and
an opportunist ("she didn't say it in her four-page statement, but ... she
said it yesterday").[85] The edited scene in the film has compressed and
rearranged the actual transcript material to make this logical progression
emphatic. In the transcript of the proceedings Hatch brings up finding *The
Exorcist* as the source of the allegation before mentioning the investigators
trying to dig up material to damage Thomas.[86] The final note in this
progression is to reframe the very presence of Hill's family, ostensibly
there to support her, as opportunism. Hatch's statements gradually fade
out as he is commenting on Hill's family, that "they looked beautiful, they
look like wonderful people to me. Look at her parents, they are clearly
good people, clearly, her sisters, clearly good people. But I saw the
entourage come in, and I'm not saying they did this, but can bet your
bottom dollar that someone found every possible stereotype, to use your
terms."

The interplay between public and private events in the scene emphasizes
and clarifies how the procedural logic of the hearing favors the preferences
of power, as well as illuminating how power stems from what can be
constructed before the public. Hatch is responding to statements Hill
made previously. In this procedure Hill and other women who would
provide evidence to support her claims are suppressed precisely because
what they are saying has been cast in the perspective of abusing the
nominee. The committee's procedural exclusions state, essentially, that
what happens in private space should remain there. Hill is never given the
opportunity to respond to Hatch's claims before the committee. The
structure of the scene juxtaposes the assertion that Hill opportunely has
brought up the plagiarized Coke can story with Hill only able to reassert
her victimization in the limited privacy of her hotel suite. Even worse, she

is allowed only in this scene to do so through the even more confining, more private space of a telephone call, a call that can only offer the consolation that "it's politics, truth hardly enters into it."

A second strategy the film uses to frame the interaction of documentary record and response is to theatricalize public space in order to project onto the outer world the interior action the words in the hearing transcripts connote. In these instances (they recur several times in the film) the testimonies Hill and Thomas present adhere to the statements the two made before the committee, but the setting of the reenactment shifts into an abstract space of mood and emotion. It is here we see Hill's anguish, and Thomas most explicitly visualized as performing the victim he is claiming to be. One example to show how this functions will suffice: in the film's chronology this is Thomas's turn before the committee just before Hatch rises to his defense (while in fact, approximately 45 pages of transcript separate the two appearances). Thomas begins by saying "unequivocally, uncategorically that I deny each and every single allegation against me today that suggested in any way that I had conversations of a sexual nature or about pornographic material with Anita Hill, that I ever attempted to date her, that I ever had any personal sexual interest in her, or that I in any way ever harassed her."[87] As he speaks, the chamber's normal, hard, high-key lighting dims to spotlight Thomas's upturned palms. Addressing a darkened chamber, he stands, approaches the committee table, and removes his shirt, leaving his tie around his neck. He continues:

> I think something is dreadfully wrong with this country, when any person, any person in this free country would be subject to this. This is not a closed room.
> ... There was an FBI investigation. This is not an opportunity to talk about difficult matters privately or in a closed environment. This is a circus. It is a national disgrace. And from my standpoint, as a black American, as far as I am concerned, it is a high-tech lynching for uppity blacks who in any way deign to think for themselves, to do for themselves, to have different ideas, and it is a message that, unless you kow-tow to an old order, this is what will happen to you, you will be lynched, destroyed, caricatured by a committee of the U.S. Senate, rather than hung from a tree.[88]

As Thomas describes the confirmation process as a way of lynching an uppity black, he lifts up the end of his necktie, turning it into a hangman's noose, and the word "lynching" echoes three times. Along with the shifts in lighting, costume, and action, these theatricalized adaptations of the transcript incorporate extreme, emphatic readings of the lines of testimony, so that the performance foregrounds the oldness of the "old order," and Thomas's incredulity that this is being exposed publicly.

The film's construction of these confrontations illuminates the interplay between public and private space. *Strange Justice*'s interaction of documentary and re-created material clarifies emphatically how the processes of spin compete to frame the roles of victim and victimizer. *The Exorcist* scene foregrounds Hatch's advocacy by allowing his presence in documentary material to interact with re-created representations of disempowered response, while the theatricalization of Thomas's testimony shows his assumption of the victim role explicitly as performance. Both interplays illustrate how the storyteller in the spotlight seizes the power of definition. The film serves as a timely reminder of the consequences of the unprecedented conservative control of the media exercised by the two terms of the Bush administration, as well as its opportunities to seat on the Supreme Court John Roberts, as successor to Chief Justice William Rehnquist, and Samuel Alito to replace retiring Justice Sandra Day O'Connor. Meanwhile the array of organizations, interest groups, and lobbyists ready, willing, and able to engage in the combat of spin and counterspin have become a matter of public record.[89] *Strange Justice* argues emphatically and explicitly that spin remains the weapon of choice in the holy war of politics. The warriors are storytellers in its view of this particular chapter of American jurisprudery. It shows the campaign to nominate and confirm Thomas as a power play staged by storytellers, and shows how stories exert power when their claims, as well as their telling, not only write the script and cast the parts but also set the stage and occupy it exclusively.

CHAPTER EIGHT

THIS TIME IT'S PERSONAL:
THE ETHICS OF 9/11 DOCUDRAMA

> "The film had no script at all, just a rough
> outline that the director Paul Greengrass
> laid out for us as a 'road map' of the actual
> facts known."
> —David Alan Basche, actor (Todd Beamer
> in *United 93*)[90]

While Paul Greengrass's *United 93* (2006) differs markedly from *Strange Justice* in substance and style, it shares the movie-of-the-week's interest in exploring and explaining the public spectacle that arises from the clash of political ambition and its constraints. In performing their true stories in the arena of political events both films focus on how the explosion into public view of constrained personal, political desire translates into public knowledge, imprinting itself indelibly in public memory.

Part of the evil brilliance of the events of 9/11 is that they were conceived as spectacle. The terrorism of 9/11 endures as it recurs in images seared into our memories and cultural imagination.

The impact of important historical events, magnified further by the power and ubiquity of their spectacular images, guarantees the interest of Hollywood. Equally inevitable will be the ethical implications of treating these events through feature films. This chapter focuses on *United 93* to examine how its re-creation of the hijacking of one of the 9/11 aircraft responds to the question of the morality of its storytelling. As a 9/11 docudrama *United 93* is both similar to and different from Oliver Stone's *World Trade Center* (2006) in viewing world-altering events on the scale of personal space rather than political dynamics. *United 93* argues that comprehending the terror of 9/11 terrorism must begin with confronting the fear of what we can only imagine about the horror of that day. The challenge morally for any 9/11 docudrama is to tell the stories of true people and events without distortion or emotional exploitation.

As feature films and movies-of-the-week based on true stories, docudramas generally raise two interrelated ethical concerns. The first tends to focus on questions of fidelity. How valid—how proper—is the work's contribution to history? What does it contribute (and how) to our understanding of the past? A concern for "fidelity" considers the accuracy of record, but at the same time recognizes the limits of what "accuracy" entails. Any record will be circumscribed by the time, place, and means of its creation, as well as the terms of its reception. How does a work claim to correspond with what it represents? How true to the "true story" is what we're seeing on the screen? Did these events really occur "this way"? Is this really the history it purports to be? In previous work discussing the ethics of docudrama, I focused on the problem of fidelity in terms of the "proximity" of a work to the sources upon which it is based.[91] For a work to be "based on" a true story suggests that it faces a moral obligation to maintain a close basis to the variety of historical materials that allow its story to be told.

The second concern is related to form. Is a feature film or a movie-of-the week an appropriate means of presentation? Should the material of history, people who lived and acted and events that occurred, appear before us through the codes and conventions of classic Hollywood storytelling and melodrama that are characteristic of docudrama?[92] Is it ethical to represent sober actuality through a medium that purports to entertain? Is it proper to render the complexity of an individual's life through the conventions—the rules and expectations—of characterization that govern feature film storytelling? Can the structure of a two-hour story that develops and resolves major and minor dramatic conflicts serve properly the multifaceted, often contradictory views of events historical records represent?

The ethical questions and concerns that docudramas raise become more acute in proportion to the importance and the notoriety of the subject matter the works re-create. One need look no further than responses to the "outlaw history" of the Kennedy assassination Oliver Stone proposes in *JFK* (1991), or critics' concerns over the "sentimental" treatment of the Holocaust Steven Spielberg offers us in *Schindler's List* (1993).[93]

Feature films and movies-of-the-week based on "true stories" of September 11 will be subject to the same kind of scrutiny. The events of 9/11 remain lived history for the audiences of works that examine the impact of that day. The enormity of those events only heightens the importance of the historical fidelity and structural appropriateness of works purporting to depict them.

In the summer of 2006, the first two major Hollywood productions to re-create the terrorism of 9/11 appeared in theaters, *United 93* and *World Trade Center*. Although the films both tell stories about individuals caught up in the events of that day, the conventionality of *World Trade Center* puts it on different ground, ethically, from the more documentary visual style and collective development of character groups in *United 93*. *United 93* focuses on the hijacking of the one airliner that did not reach its designated target.   *World Trade Center* re-creates the fate of two firefighters trapped beneath the rubble of the collapsed World Trade Center (WTC) buildings and makes traditional use of melodrama as a narrative framework, centering on victims and their families as a means to moralize about the fates of its characters. The restricted focus of both films favors a personal, rather than a larger, political view of 9/11 terrorism. The films argue that our understanding of the impact of 9/11 begins with this restricted focus on the experiences of individuals, and, by extension, our own reactions to those stories.

As it takes this focus, these films, and 9/11 docudrama generally, will raise the following questions: Is a more personal approach to storytelling a useful and appropriate means of creating an understanding of these events and these people? Do these films have a responsibility to explore further the larger contexts that frame their stories?   Should they risk alienating either the Republican or Democratic half of a potential American audience, for example, by addressing the political implications of the failure of leadership 9/11 revealed? Is it sufficient to confine the United 93 story to the actions we see, as a way of understanding why these people, as opposed to those on three other aircraft, were able to resist? Is *United 93's* categorical view of those involved, its withholding of names and the conventions of individualized characterization, an asset to the larger purposes of its storytelling? Is it appropriate—not just aesthetically, but also morally—to confine our understanding of these victims to these portrayals? Has the speculative humanizing of the United 93 hijackers allowed the film to venture onto morally questionable ground? Does a restricted scope of representation enhance or limit remembrance? Does the sense of access to events through Hollywood storytelling adequately serve their magnitude? Is this kind of representation the best way to remember, allowing an appropriate memorial to victims and survivors?

Re-creating the fates of 9/11 victims in Hollywood feature films heightens even further the ethical challenges to docudrama, because these are commercial works made to be sold to as many viewers as possible.

The ethical questions of 9/11 docudrama arise as these stories perform the momentous events of 9/11 in re-creating the actions of individuals.

The emphasis on the personal space of key figures allows performance to provide both a means of access to history as well as the opportunity to confront the fears that history elicits. Docudramatic performance in these works must account for both the fundamental ethical concerns of fidelity and appropriateness. We are offered performances that are modeled on the known, bringing the result in close proximity to the historical record. As performance in personal space reenacts and reclaims the time and space of the real, it affords the opportunity to frame the terror that, at bottom, is the goal of terrorism.

Fidelity: Addressing What We Know

Both *United 93* and *World Trade Center* presume their viewers have shared the 9/11 "experience" as members of a media audience. As different as they are in scope and style, both films address the surrealism of our encounter with 9/11 as a media creation. That experience is probably typified by the almost inestimable repetition of several traumatic images. These include images of the penetration and eruption of the towers, and their nightmarish, slow-motion collapses. Broadcast repetition of these images remains our initial and perhaps one of our more definitive means of access to the actual. Each repetition asserts "this actually happened" but does so, ironically, in this dream-like way. Repetition must be the reference point for "experiencing" what happened, whether on one of the planes, at Ground Zero, in one of the control towers, or in the WTC itself. Michael Moore in *Fahrenheit 9/11* (2004) appears to have decided that we can all relive that mediated trauma without having to show it exactly that way again, and that it's only necessary to refer to it to re-evoke it. Moore does so, however, with black screens, shocked, upturned faces, and repeated images of sheets of paper, cascading like confetti in the air around the towers.

With that cultural vision as a given reference point, *United 93* and *World Trade Center* share a common persuasive strategy—that the reality of the 9/11 experience is accessible by claiming personal space as public. Both argue for the "truth" of their stories through fear appeals that characterize the physical space occupied by the main characters as claustrophobic. Both films render the space of their settings as constricted and oppositional. The plane cabin on United 93 offers minimal terrain, with its seats and aisles, shut doors, and slim opportunities, not to mention the confined drama danced out on the monitor screens and through the windows in various control rooms. The rubble in *World Trade Center* kills, with its masses of concrete, twisted pipe, sparking wires, and the impossibly small gaps left for human remains. In emphasizing the claustrophobic both films convert America's experience of terrorists and terrorism to the specific and personal. *United 93* and *World Trade Center* strive to persuade us that when we view the enormity of 9/11's public events through constricted, claustrophobic, visceral images, what we see has a meaning for us that is direct, immediate, and personal, rather than abstract, ideological, and mythic.

Greengrass approaches the contested space of his docudramas, *Bloody Sunday* (2002) and *United 93*, as one would a chessboard, in which the space of action puts the rules of engagement into play, and the principals are comparable to all the pieces from kings to pawns. *Bloody Sunday* concentrates on several groups of characters whose functions in the actual events depicted arise from their desires to move within and control the streets of Derry. These groups include: the protest leaders debating whether or not to march for their civil rights and their supporters; the youth of Derry who join the march and are the particular target of the British troops there to control the city; the soldiers themselves, who are characterized as preoccupied first with how violent they should be, and then with how to cover up the consequences of their violence; and the officers in command of the troops who constantly compare wall-mounted street maps tracing the march and the placement of troops against radio-relayed information about the unfolding conflict. Re-creating these events extends outward from what characters desire to the environment in which the consequences of their decisions are enacted. We see the wall map, then the streets filled with combatants, then hear the information from observers both above and within those same streets. The film's emphasis on space and how it is structured continually underlines the modeling of events, and argues for the authenticity—the fidelity—of its depiction.

The "Truth" of Terror

United 93 similarly addresses the 9/11 experience of its audience by focusing not on the terrorism that precipitated the events of that day, but by re-creating the places of terror of both victims and perpetrators. Although terrorism's impact on events and lives provides the premise of the story, we are not offered any kind of socio-political analysis of terrorism. Both *United 93* and *World Trade Center* argue for the fidelity of their representations by working emphatically with the settings of 9/11 terrorism. The buildings, work places, and modes of transportation—the visible surface of what is normally innocent and everyday—are turned by that day's terrorism into tools of destruction.

United 93's settings become claustrophobic as it examines the three, interrelated experiences of terror that develop this particular chapter of 9/11. We see the story of the doomed flight from the perspectives of the hijackers, the passengers, and the flight controllers. From the microcosmic experiences of these three groups, we are to view the destructive, ideological commitment of the perpetrators, the heroic resistance of their victims, and the inadequate preparation of the professionals in charge of airline security.

United 93 operates in somewhat the same way as a snuff film. The film's purpose is to deliver a known outcome, building interest by developing the horror of the moments before death. We know the fate of the people on the flight before the film even begins. A snuff film, however, would exploit the prurient appeal of the moment that an actual life is extinguished (see for example, the popularity of online videos of the Daniel Pearl beheading, or the hanging of Saddam Hussein[94]). *United 93* re-creates this particular chapter of 9/11 in order to make the moment of impending doom accessible. Staging the last hours of the doomed crew and passengers imagines the unimaginable for an audience that may now relive vicariously what "it" must have been like—what it must have been like to prepare and execute the attack, what it must have been like for passengers and attendants to have this violence erupt out of the mundane routine of a cross-country flight, and what it must have been like to have the strict procedures of domestic air traffic go bad so quickly.

The film depends upon two basic strategies to create and sustain the atmosphere of doom it explores. First, *United 93* unfolds in approximately the same amount of elapsed time as the events it re-creates. Consequently, the opening image showing Jarrah, the hijacker who will pilot the plane, at morning prayers in his hotel room, is tantamount to lighting the fuse of a two-hour time bomb. We know what will happen and approximately when. The film's real-time chronology indicates the lengths to which Greengrass's production went in maintaining the closest possible proximity to what was known about the events it re-creates. Interviews with Greengrass and reviews of the film make much of the production's work with its source material, drawing not only on the chronology graphed out in *The 9/11 Commission Report*, but also upon the cockpit recordings, the transcripts of the calls passengers made, and the extensive interviews with the recipients of those calls, other family members, and the professionals involved in the events depicted.[95]

The second strategy the film develops is to show doomed passengers through images that are relentlessly claustrophobic. The tight limits of the visual world of the film echo appropriately the closed fate of its principals.

This imagery grows in part out of *United 93*'s reliance upon elements of documentary style. In addition to casting unknown or relatively low-profile actors as passengers and hijackers, many of those in the roles of professionals are doing in the film what they do in life, including the air traffic controllers, some of whom play themselves in the film.[96] Here, and in his earlier work in *Bloody Sunday*, Greengrass has shown his roots in the British drama-documentary tradition.[97] The images showing how these people respond to the situation rapidly changing around them are in the vein of direct cinema, shot with hand-held cameras, shifting quickly with the flow of information, and maintaining a tight, conversational proximity to the actors.[98] As viewers we are wedged visually into the same situations as the people we see on screen.

The film shifts between two kinds of worlds. We see the work areas of various civil and military air traffic control rooms in Virginia, up-state New York, Boston, Newark, Cleveland, and Indianapolis. These alternate with the surroundings of those boarding the plane. Once the control rooms are established the story becomes confined to events graphically rendered on arrays of monitors, and the reactions of those trying to make sense of and cope with what they see there. The many shots of the passengers on the plane emphasize the mundane, universal nature of the experience of flying, confining action to the areas in and around seats, and the aisle of the plane. The passengers read, work, eat, and converse. The flight attendants engage in their routines within and around their work stations. In all cases the film constricts its story to personal space bound by the physical limits of the setting. As events develop, all of these normally innocent elements take on new meaning as they become oppositional, and the space of events constricts into the space of confrontation.

The Propriety of Storytelling Form:
The Melodrama of Fear

By contrast, *World Trade Center* establishes and then shifts away from necessarily tight shots of its trapped characters, to allow them (and us) the opportunity to escape into the space of memory. Through the film's flashback structure we see the two main characters, Jimeno (Michael Pena) and McLaughlin (Nicolas Cage), in bed with their wives, or playing with their children. The flashbacks suggest that memory provides both relief from the crushing reality of the physical space that constrains them, and motivation to live by reinforcing what is most meaningful to the men.

World Trade Center develops its story through a traditional melodramatic structure, building on the configurations possible because of vulnerable, self-sacrificing characters victimized by destructive physical and social settings. The return to the unrestricted space of normal life at the conclusion of the story suggests not only resolution of the conflict we have seen unfold, but also an affirmation of the moral system the film's story serves. The virtuous triumph through their survival. The film's closure has a sense of ethical incongruity; it is a 9/11 story with a happy ending.

Alternatively, the three groups of characters in *United 93* replace the conventional, individual characters that provide the customary comforts of a dramatic, classical Hollywood narrative film. Greengrass has remained emphatic about how the film's "collective" approach to its characters was both fundamental to the project's creative process, and necessary for understanding how the passengers came to take the action they did as a group.[99] Individuals become reference points for us within these groups. However who they are as people—this is not a film that uses or reinforces names, for example—remains secondary to how we see them respond to the building confrontation. Their similar, yet differing responses create the film's identification strategies.

Since it is a story in which death is certain, *United 93* foregrounds its killers. The four terrorists provide one of the most consistent, unifying elements of the dramatic structure of the film. Unlike the controllers or passengers the terrorists are present in every stage of *United 93*'s narrative development. Taken together, as four members of a group, the hijackers contribute an arc of character development following what classical Hollywood narrative conventions require to establish, build, and resolve conflict. They develop from a preparatory stage (morning prayers, followed by the passage through airport security) that marks both what they desire and what might oppose it, continuing through the wait that leads up to the attack, and climaxing with the attack on the plane itself and its resolution. Even though we are never offered the opportunity to learn anything about the hijackers as individuals, actions that signal their different kinds of apprehension serve to individualize them.[100] The pilot prays. The co-pilot reads. The third hijacker appears the most agitated, nervously leaving his seat to demand from the hijacker pilot that the time has come. The bomber hunches into his zipped jacket and clutches his flight bag.

United 93's consistent return to and emphasis on the emotions of the hijackers strives to humanize, rather than demonize them. The stress of their pending suicides illustrates their relatable fears of both failure and success. This forms one of the film's dramatic cornerstones.

Against this line of development, *United 93* compiles what one might expect to be the film's preferred area of identification, a growing familiarity with the plane's passengers and flight attendants. This group remains less individualized, however. As the story returns to a few of them, they become reference points. One of the attendants[101] calls United and reports the hijacking. Subsequently she is allowed to tend briefly to a mortally stabbed passenger, and move up the cabin and back to relay information. One of the male passengers, a younger man in a baseball cap,[102] reacts first by attempting to flee, and then helps lead the fight. One of the businessmen[103] speaks for most of the others and helps provoke their resistance. Their story also develops in a group arc. They grow from everyday innocence to progressive awareness, not only of their immediate situation, but also of the larger events of 9/11 and their place in it. Knowledge culminates in an understanding that they will need to fight back in order to have a chance to survive.

United 93's development of the air traffic controllers as a third character group focuses, ironically, on their spiraling loss of control. The arc of their development is their transformation from informed "insiders," the group that should be and strives to be in control, to increasingly helpless witnesses. The controllers are not even present in the last stage of the story. Consequently the film renders the controllers' experience of that 9/11 morning in a way that visually approximates our own, underlining their status as bystanders, viewers of events in which they should have greater agency.

As with the hijackers and plane occupants, several individuals within the group of controllers function as reference points. Most notably, Ben Sliney, playing himself, becomes the face of institutional frustration as he tries to patrol the point position in the Federal Aviation Administration's national center in Herndon, Virginia. Sliney is one of the only characters in *United 93* given a name, however, his function in the story is limited to what he is supposed to do and what he can't do in his job.   Sliney maintains his professionalism, embodying the need to adhere to procedure even when procedure deteriorates under a barrage of information and misinformation. We see Sliney's counterparts in the military equally frustrated when flights vary from their routes and radio patterns, and begin to crash into targets on the Eastern seaboard.

The film repeatedly emphasizes the controllers' 9/11 experience as one of viewing. Shots alternate briskly between the aircraft icons on air traffic screens and the controllers watching and commenting on what they see there. The film also renders through screens how the controllers, like us, must watch 9/11's climactic moments. The airport control tower window at Newark has a view of the burning WTC towers that resembles a large screen TV. Sliney's group is watching CNN monitors when the second plane strikes the South Tower. So are the military responsible for the air space over Manhattan and Washington, D.C. Everyone in these rooms gasps in horror, their reaction mirroring the responses of everyone else watching the events on television at that moment. To show the experience of the air traffic controllers as helpless, distanced viewers emphasizes the helplessness we all felt as we watched.

In *World Trade Center* it is the families waiting for news that provide viewpoint and consequently the film's key identification opportunities. The film's concentration on waiting families, summed up by the image(s) of the "missing" posted on the bulletin board in the hospital cafeteria where relatives have been told to wait, visualizes the impact of events in the domestic terms of melodrama. The film repeatedly turns to view the aftermath of the collapsed towers from the perspectives of anxious, extended families. The Jimenos disagree on what the name of the new baby will be. The McLaughlins' younger son castigates his mother for not getting down to the site and searching the rubble. In sum, the attack on the WTC, in the view of the film, is best understood as an attack on families.

A Moral Argument for Heroism

As *United 93* integrates documentary material and the narrative strategies of melodrama, the film's three basic character configurations provide the structure for moral argument. The moral implications of victims striving to take heroic action develop within a narrative built on cornerstones of suicidal commitment, belated but necessary resistance, and frustrated professionalism. Melodrama in film tends to focus on victims of repressive circumstances in order to clarify the moral ramifications of the interactions between individual and context, desire and setting. *United 93* situates its known, documentary material within these parameters. Both news reports at the time[104] and *The 9/11 Commission Report* defined the primary victims, the crew and passengers, as heroes for succeeding in preventing the plane from reaching its intended target (the Capitol building in Washington, D.C., as the photo the pilot clips to the control console would suggest). The film shows that as their realization of larger events grows, the passengers act primarily out of self-preservation. They know planes have crashed into the WTC, but have no idea of what the intended target of their flight might be. What is heroic is their willingness to fight back in the face of evident obstacles. The film's argument is visual. It equates ethical action with the loss of physical space. Courage increases as space constricts to the narrow door to the cockpit, the last and most impenetrable obstacle to self-preservation.

The controllers are secondary victims, but suffer from the ineffectiveness of the procedures and protocols of their profession. They are victimized both by their commitment to their professional training, and the tools they have to live up to its obligations. The visual concentration on the overwhelming flow of information from monitors and phone calls, and the exchanges of this information between control centers, underlines how the circumstances were, in the terms of *The 9/11 Commission Report*, "unprecedented," suggesting the system's inadequate preparation for such events.[105] The repeated images of the hijackers in prayer before and after they launch their attack suggests that this group of characters has been victimized by the destructiveness of its ideological commitment. We see this strictly as an aspect of character. Why this extreme religious belief would compel these (and the other) 9/11 hijackers to this most extreme kind of action is clearly not within the scope of the film's exploration of the event.

United 93 rigorously concentrates its view of the repressive circumstances that create victims on the immediate, visually constrained surroundings of the plane and the control centers, emphasizing how the principal players performed within those spaces of constricted possibilities. The energy of the film's narrative is focused not so much on what larger causes doomed the victims, but on what the experience of that doom must have been like.

Evoking Memory Ethically

What kind of understanding results, then, from the docudramatic performance of United 93's history? The answer Greengrass's film proposes is this: Before 9/11, for most Americans the experience of terrorism was largely an abstraction, events reported in other parts of the world that happened to other people. Living 9/11 indirectly, through reported, mediated events, brought the experience of terrorism closer both geographically and personally with the incessant repetition of the traumatic images that form the iconography of 9/11: the striking of the towers, towers enflamed, bodies falling from great heights, and perhaps the most relatable images of all, the hopelessness of passengers on doomed airliners. As we re-inflict this with each re-imagining of what the claustrophobic finality of United 93 must have been like, we relive the very terror the perpetrators desired us to suffer.

Several reviewers of the film have faulted this approach, shown from the perspective of groups, rather than conventionally individualized protagonists, for failing to allow the possibility of a cathartic experience.[106] This critical position rests upon two assumptions, that the film's re-creation aims at catharsis, and that a cathartic effect must result from our identification with the desires of individual characters.

The first assumption addresses the event as tragedy. Certainly the story of those tragically doomed to death on United 93 creates the opportunity to purge pity and fear. However, there is a difference when the story re-creates the fates of real-life individuals, rather than literary characters. The grounding of the United 93 story in actuality makes the process of imagining the unimaginable closer to a secondary memory than to the identification strategies of literary characterization.[107] None of us might have been on United 93, but in reliving the terror of the experience as if we were, we create for ourselves a posttraumatic, secondary memory of what it "must" have been like. Given that what we see is grounded in the actuality that creates the sense of terror for us, the first function of *United 93*'s storytelling will be to confront the event as a source of fear.

The second assumption also grows out of the conventions of character development in feature film. We identify customarily with individual characters. In this case is it appropriate to do so? Characterization in *United 93* suggests an alternative and arguably ethical choice in avoiding the potential emotional exploitation that could result from portraying actual individuals as characters we should identify with. It is the very unconventionality of *United 93*'s group characters, coupled with its shifting, hand-held, direct cinema shooting style, that allows the style of storytelling to evoke the experience of posttraumatic memory.

Film has the capacity to evoke traumatic experience when representation finds alternatives to the conventions of realism. Janet Walker defines "trauma cinema" as "films that deal with a world-shattering event or events, whether public or personal … in a nonrealist mode characterized by a disturbance and fragmentation of the films' narrative and stylistic regimes."[108] It is necessary to do so, Walker suggests, to model effectively the memory of traumatic experience "by drawing on innovative strategies for representing reality obliquely, by looking to mental processes for inspiration, and by incorporating self-reflexive devices to call attention to the friability of the scaffolding for audiovisual historiography"[109] *United 93*'s performance of collective experiences, shot in a documentary style, foregrounds the film's processes of re-creating traumatic events.

Strictly conventional means of representation imply that traumatic experience can, and perhaps should, be contained by the sense of control and closure of classic Hollywood narrative form. The "happy ending" of *World Trade Center* argues for this kind of containment through the release of its main characters, their return to their families, and the epilogue's suggestion that their lives now go on. In order to confront traumatic experience, rather than repress its disturbing effect, the films that "invite a posttraumatic historical consciousness" blend the strategies of conventional realism and the formal provocations of modernism.[110] Such films belong to a "discourse of trauma," texts that arise after a traumatizing historical event and attempt to represent its often unrepresentable nature.

The ethical aim of film in this instance is:

> … to overcome defensive numbing. Documentary images must be submitted to a narrative discourse the purpose of which is, if not to literally traumatize the spectator, at least to invoke a posttraumatic historical consciousness—a kind of textual compromise between the senselessness of the initial traumatic encounter and the sense-making apparatus of a fully integrated historical narrative.[111]

Joshua Hirsch suggests that "posttraumatic cinema" evokes the traumatic experience but in a context that strives to "make sense" of it.[112] In Hirsch's view conventional historical narrative contains trauma too neatly, conveying the erroneous impression that it has been controlled in the telling. Making sense of trauma in a constructive way, in a way that will frame it without defusing it, requires a self-conscious narrative—that is, a narrative that can accommodate calling attention to its own processes:

> Posttraumatic memory may not be self-conscious *per se*. But insofar as posttraumatic memory is a kind of failure of memory, its therapeutic treatment requires a degree of self-consciousness that is uncharacteristic of narrative memory.[113]

By adhering to unconventional strategies of characterization in performing the experiences of the groups whose story we see, and by foregrounding both dramatic and cinematic performance as a model of the process of memory, *United 93* aims for confrontation with the unthinkable and unrepresentable, rather than with the conventions of cathartic realism.

United 93's performance of people and events is both modeled on and directly linked to the actuality it represents. Consequently it allows the access to the real that Hirsch and Walker suggest can be one of the main goals of the process of dealing with traumatic history. By identifying and confronting the source of fear, it becomes possible to short-circuit the compulsive reliving of the experience of terror.

United 93 does not address directly the larger social, political, economic, and cultural forces at work in the events of 9/11. If it limits its re-creation to one flight's passengers, hijackers, and flight controllers, its docudramatic framework provides the first and most personally relevant kind of understanding of its subject for any of us, an understanding that is an essential prerequisite for a further reckoning with the larger issues of the sources of terrorism. As we relive the finality of United 93 the film's performance of the real shows us that these were people, like us, and that confronting the terror that terrorism creates must begin with the personal.

CHAPTER NINE

DOCUDRAMATIZING THE EVENTS OF WAR: *DEFIANCE* AND *FLAGS OF OUR FATHERS*

Re-creating the events of war remains a staple of Hollywood genre production, however it offers us a second, significant arena within which features and movies-of-the week portray actual people and events, perform the past, and shape public memory of key figures, their deeds, and the repercussions. Within the range of eras and conflicts these films re-create, the chapters that follow will discuss docudramas about World War II (*Defiance*; *Flags of Our Fathers*; *Uprising*; *The Pianist*; *Nuremberg*); Vietnam (*We Were Soldiers*); incursions of the 90s (*Black Hawk Down*); and Iraq (*Saving Jessica Lynch*). In each case war docudramas operate within the most visceral kinds of arenas. This chapter returns to the concept of the arena of representation in examining how *Defiance* foregrounds its forest setting in order to argue for a revised public memory of Jewish resistance during the Holocaust. Memory becomes more explicitly the subject of *Flags of Our Fathers,* a film that meditates upon memory, as it explores the clash of various (and various kinds of) personal memories with the creation of public memory.

A comparison of *Flags of Our Fathers* (C. Eastwood, 2006) and *Defiance* (E. Zwick, 2008) offers an instructive case study in the role of docudramatic performance in shaping public memory. Both films are Hollywood feature film docudramas, made by prominent directors no strangers to making films "based on true stories" with star casts and comfortable budgets. Both are World War II docudramas with stories rooted in different theaters of war but centered on the viscerality of combat. In both films their settings function as arenas, as I will discuss in detail below. In *Flags* setting frames the problem of memory, as the film argues that the key issue in our public memory of the flag raising on Mount Suribachi is a matter of how various kinds of memory intersect. *Defiance* urges that we remember its characters and events as a matter of the attitude summed up in its title. In *Defiance* the film's setting frames the materiality of memory. *Defiance* roots its arguments in the texture and tangibility of its primary setting, the forest, as it stages the action we see. Thus it shapes our view of the memory of the action (the defiance; the resistance) it re-creates. In *Defiance* the materiality of the memory the film performs works to counter the iconographic view of more urban Jewish resistance and survival in the Holocaust evident in docudramas such as *Schindler's List*, *The Pianist*, and *Uprising*. Writing in *Variety* critic Todd McCarthy went even further, noting "'Defiance' seems explicitly designed to counter the prevailing image of Jews acquiescing to their fates in ghettos and camps without fighting back."[114] To assert a counter memory of "defiance" this film offers instead images of Jews living and fighting in the forest. The idea of the reciprocal legibility of performance and the stage that frames it is evident in how both films emphasize setting in arguing for their respective contributions to public memory of their subjects.

Defiance

In Zwick's *Defiance*, the forest defines the arena within which this story of the past occurs and becomes present for us. The film's cinematographer envisioned the presence of the forest by depicting it as a "smothering character."[115] The logline for *Defiance* could be, quite simply, "in World War II, displaced Belorussian Jews live and fight in the woods." We see the ultimate evil of the prior acts that initiate the story encapsulated in the first few minutes of the film, as apparently documentary images of people—Jews—being rounded up from cities and villages, shot at random and executed next to ditches, dissolve into the color "present" of the film's story. The enormity of the evil that precipitates the film's events becomes counterbalanced in the story we see by the necessity—the propriety—of corrective action. Three examples from *Defiance* illustrate how we have to read action in the film as a product of setting. The reciprocal legibility of action and setting show how the forest and specifically its trees function as an arena in the film. These examples focus on the actions of building, grieving, and fighting. Each action contributes to the construction of identity, makes the past present, and shapes for us what public memory scholar Allison Landsberg calls our "prosthetic memory" of character and events.[116]

After a substantial group of refugees has formed within the Bielski's forest encampment, we see a scene involving two of the brothers, Tuvia (Daniel Craig) and Zus (Liev Schrieber), and Isaac (Mark Feuerstein), constructing the frames for shelters out of tree limbs and trunks. As the scene opens Isaac drops his hammer nearly striking Zus, who asks him,

"What is it you do?" Isaac explains that he "was—am—an intellectual," and had published a "journal," well actually, he explains, it was really more of a pamphlet. Zus replies, "This is a job?" Another Bielski relative walks by a moment later to introduce the men to his "forest wife." In this scene trees provide construction material, as well as the means to redefine and reinvent new roles in a new society. As the self-professed intellectual struggles to become a carpenter his former work with paper has left him ill-prepared to use a hammer. The past exists in talk and thoughts; the present exists in action; the scene indicates the need for effective action with the existing tools and materials the group has at hand. Action (building; taking on a different spouse) frames identity.

Shortly after this scene Zus finds out that his wife and child have in all likelihood been murdered during the purging of their town. He staggers several steps, collapses to his knees, and repeatedly slams his head against the trunk of a tree until Tuvia embraces him from behind to stop him. The tree he pounds his forehead against becomes, in effect, not only the cause of grief, a stand-in for the larger wall Jewish life has run up against in the early 40s in Belorussia, but also the means to express and purge grief. The tree trunk becomes the measure of his agony and strength. The action indicates that both his grief and his endurance are as strong as the tree itself. The blood on his head—the visible evidence of loss—persists through the next several scenes, functioning as an indicator of his identity, as well as marking the materiality of memory—his of his wife and child, ours (now) of the pain and effort life in the forest necessitates.

To repay their loss of family the Bielskis exact revenge on Nazis and their sympathizers. As a direct consequence of Zus's grief, he declares that now it is his turn to do what Tuvia did earlier, to seek an "eye for an eye" retribution. Now a band of partisans, the Bielski group launches a night attack in the forest first against a passing enemy motorcyclist, then the escorted car that comes shortly behind it, and then engages the truck full of soldiers that comes just minutes behind the staff car. The trees in the scene provide cover for their attacks. The forest is more important in the scene now as their turf, the space they need to defend. The film shows the attacks to be preemptive and proactive, since the enemy that transgresses the forest in which the Jews now live needs to be eliminated. The scene's justification of preemptive action—showing how the best defense is a good offense—makes the past present but with the ideological repercussions and reinforcement that must accompany seeing Jews launch preemptive attacks against an enemy that would annihilate them. *Chicago Sun Times* critic Roger Ebert noticed the analogy to present-day politics, describing the brothers' dilemma as a conflict between "helping our side or harming theirs."[117] The fact that they—we—are in the forest in the first place reminds us that the enormity of evil that creates the world of the film places preemptive action on moral higher ground, while avoiding the moral problematic preemptive actions create in contemporary Israeli politics and within the dynamics of Jewish identity.

Flags of Our Fathers and the Performance of Memory

Flags of Our Fathers, the first of two films Clint Eastwood released in 2006 recreating the Battle of Iwo Jima, centers on many of the traditional concerns of the World War II combat film. In re-creating the hellish viscerality of the extended combat for the tiny island the film examines thoroughly the costs of victory, survival, and the nature of heroism. As it looks back at events of more than six decades ago, *Flags* also becomes a film about memory. We come to understand memory as the performance of the past.

The film adapts James Bradley's book researching the role his father played as one of the soldiers who raised the American flag over the island. The photograph of that moment taken by news photographer Joe Rosenthal immediately became an icon of the meaning of American war efforts in the South Pacific. The Rosenthal photograph accordingly becomes the subject of Bradley's book and Eastwood's feature film adaptation. Eastwood's film also centers on the book's mission, that a son, in searching for the "true story" of his father's war experiences, investigates the past. The film's representation of present-day research, past combat, and the consequences of the war examines the complexity of memory in several basic ways. First, the film reflects Bradley's research and interviews with witnesses and participants by offering their testimony as narrators of the action and events we see. The film's multiple narrators and its return repeatedly to key moments in time underline the prismatic nature of memory. Point of view shapes memory; location in space and time in turn shape viewpoint. Second, the film also shows how the primary memories of those whose story we are seeing has the spatial and temporal limits we expect of witnesses. Further, in some cases those with primary memories can't or won't remember the events of the past. Primary memories illuminate a third issue, the advent of traumatic memory as combat survivors become haunted in the present by their experiences of the past. Last, the iconic image of the flag raising evokes the force of public memory as it shapes the meaning of a moment in time. The film as whole serves to explore not only what might be important about a widely shared image, but also what its repercussions were, and ultimately why it is important to foreground through performance the effect on the present of memory's evocation of the past.

Flags of Our Fathers sees history precisely as a problem of memory. Its story unfolds within two frameworks centered on memory: a son's perspective impels his investigation into his father's reticence to talk about the war; the investigation finds what the father has tried not to remember. *Flags* inflects memory through this shift in the knowledge of successive generations. The film argues in part that the meaning of the battle of Iwo Jima became conveniently encapsulated in the core, iconographic image of the flag raising, and that what began as a photographic record of a performance quickly (and perhaps necessarily) became commodified as a recurring performance of the past. What the film foregrounds, however, is how memory is made vivid—literally brought to life—by the flag raisers' survivor guilt. The flag raisers are forced to relive the guilt of survival with each performance, each reiteration not so much of the original act of raising the American flag, but of its photograph. The key image the story deconstructs becomes situated in the film as an image not only of history, but more importantly of memory. In foregrounding history as performance, the film argues that the memory of the principals involved should, as it joins the famous, iconic, photograph of the flag raising on Iwo Jima, become a necessary part of cultural memory that now includes and relives the cost of survival.

The Joe Rosenthal photograph of the marines raising the flag on Mt. Suribachi drives the development of both *The Sands of Iwo Jima* (A. Dwan, 1949) and Eastwood's *Flags*. Both films recreate the relentlessly visceral nature of the combat on the island. The earlier film takes us through the fighting in order to culminate in the flag raising image. The image, the ending implies, will, as we know, become the sum of the struggle and sacrifice the story shows. *Flags*, in adapting James Bradley's best-selling account of his father's role as one of the flag raisers, in a sense begins where *Sands* ends. It is a film about this image, and consequently takes a causal view of it, examining the sources that coalesced at the moment the shutter was snapped, and the ripple effects of that moment captured on film. In vastly different ways both films argue for how we should understand what the image means. Coming at the conclusion of the 1949 version the raising of the flag identifies victory as the price of sacrifice. The flashback structure in *Flags* alternatively examines the photograph and its reiterations as the performance of historic action that both evokes and defines the meaning of the past as it resides in memory.

Flags shows how the Rosenthal photograph is the result of performance. More precisely, it is a document of a re-performance. The original action of putting up the flag and snapping the picture is, of course, a consequence of roles: GIs under orders put up a flag when they reach the summit; the chain of command orders a second flag be raised in order to hang onto the historic, original banner; the photographer, following the next group up the trail, manages to do his job and gets off a snapshot of the second flag raising. The famous Iwo Jima photograph is then a result of re-creating, re-performing, the original action. What follows becomes a logical extension of performing as a soldier and as a combat photographer.

As a further consequence, the photograph itself becomes recreated in countless images: it recurs in news photos, paintings, posters, stamps, events re-enactments, desserts at banquets, and ultimately, a monument. It is a case study in how an image becomes an icon. Each reiteration, each re-performance in each new setting imposes the contestation of the past— the struggle and the cost of victory at Iwo Jima—upon the conflicts, the issues of the present. We see the flag raisers as civilians who became GIs, as GIs who became flag raisers; as flag raisers who become fundraisers, and therefore as fundraisers they are forced to return to the space of the civilian world. Role and setting inform each other. Through the fusing of roles (GI/flag raisers ordered to work as fundraisers), and the incongruity of settings (combat at Iwo Jima reenacted in stadiums, city centers, and at dinners) the process of memory shows the interdependence of who these men are and where they are. When the GIs who were once civilians became flag raisers and then fundraisers, their relocation in civilian space reminds them, and us, repeatedly of the cost of their survival.

Flags situates memory within performance, arguing that each performance of the icon, each confrontation with the past now modeled in the present, returns the past, re-inflicts its trauma, reminds the survivors of those who are absent, and forces the survivors to question if it is right that they should be alive. The flashback structure in *Flags* repeatedly shows memory to be triggered by performance. Fireworks over a paper mache Mount Suribachi at Soldiers Field in Chicago become a bridge to the sounds of the mortar and artillery of the past. Screams of fans become the screams of soldiers. The voices of the wounded keep the traumas of the past vivid in the present.

The very incongruity of role actions and the locations that frame and define it show how performance triggers access to the past through memory. For Doc Bradley (Ryan Phillipe), the flashbacks that reassert the past in the present occur compulsively, modeling the experience of post-traumatic stress syndrome. The opening of the film suggests that this has been a life-long consequence, as we see Bradley as an old man, near death, collapsed on the stairs, asking "where did he go?" a question that returns him repeatedly to the disappearance and death of his buddy, Iggy, in the caves on Iwo Jima. The specific actions of climbing, reaching, and vocal cues relocate Bradley's present (a Mount Suribachi reenactment, for example) in the past, tending to the wounded, each one yelling "corpsman!" to call him to their aid. Bradley's long term strategy for dealing with the continuation of the past in his present is to deny its influence, not to respond to phone calls, to bury his war memorabilia and his Navy Cross in a trunk, not to speak, ever, of the experience to his family. For Ira Hayes (Adam Beach), the incongruity of civilian circumstances (dinners; hotel rooms; trains) reminds him constantly that he is in a space where he should not be, since he never wanted to leave the battlefield in the first place. Consequently we are to understand not only his compulsive drinking, but also his recurring issues with authority figures (those running the bond tour; the bartender who won't serve him and the police in Chicago) as responses to survival guilt. For both Bradley and Hayes, and for us as we watch their story, the consequences of memory, emphatically memory triggered by recurring performances of their defining moment atop Mt. Suribachi, is that performance creates both the need to remember and the effort to forget.

While considering the traditional issues of the war film, such as the quirks of fate that drive the outcome of combat, the value and meaning of heroism, and the personal and cultural cost of survival and victory, *Flags* offers a meditation on the meaning of memory. The film models memory as a means of understanding the elusive nature of the past. Its story unfolds as it examines what frames, motivates, and prevents memory. These factors explain the shaping of memory, and allow us to understand memory itself as performance. "Memories" may evoke the past, but understanding how memory stages action and events within the settings of the past allows the process of memory itself to become an even more indispensable tool in a search for truth.

Flags foregrounds this process in several ways: in the prismatic memories of the film's narrative frames, as a son searches for the story of his father's war experiences; in depicting the problematic, primary memories of the story's principals, who can't, or won't remember even the basic facts of a single event, including who was there and when; in evoking the scarring, traumatic, compulsive memory of combat and its cost; and in tracing the force of public memory when it seizes upon a powerful, single image of an event and chooses to invest an icon with charismatic power. *Flags* examines memory as a matter of staging. Memory is not simply a matter of who remembers, or where they are as a storyteller now in relation to where they were in the past, but also a result of what they select to disclose and how they choose to reveal it. The film's performance of memory further allows insight into what motivates memory, suggesting that memory as performance is formed, made necessary, by the irrepressible persistence of the past in the present. Just as the famous Rosenthal flag raising photograph gives a brief moment in the past a form, as the photo and its moment become replicated it folds the present back over upon the past, a past that Doc and Ira would rather forget, but when the past intrudes, the resurfacing of memory establishes the cost of denial.

Flags's vision of memory as the performance of the past also illuminates the spectrum of effects of survival. We understand the guilt of those who survived, and the flip side of guilt, the very miracle of survival itself, as the ceaseless work of memory. And it should be noted, finally, that the film's modeling of memory foregrounds how it is survival that allows a future. *Flags* remains a son's story as he strives to find the story of his father. The performance of memory, its selection, arrangement, framing, and full realization, links father and son, as the work of the son recovers what the price of the past exacted in defining who it was his father would become.

Flags and *Defiance*, two very different World War II docudramas, show us in very different ways that "acting with facts" does more than simply perform the past, but more importantly offers us a performance of memory. The films further show us the importance of understanding acting with facts as performance within the arenas that frame the past. The arena of the forest in *Defiance* shows us how the reciprocal legibility of action and setting shapes public memory; the contrasting arenas for performing the past in *Flags* allow us the opportunity to meditate upon how the performance of memory makes present our sense of personal and cultural identity.

CHAPTER TEN

A FEELING FOR HISTORY:
RECOVERING THE PAST
WITH SENSIBLE EVIDENCE

Provoking public memory and shaping national identity are two important functions of historical film. Docudrama contributes to a third purpose, the recovery of sentiment as a matter of history, through the foregrounding of the physical and emotional as evidence. On-screen feeling becomes instructive, qualifying for the material of history, but within the moral perspective that docudrama advocates. When narratives based on true stories make history "sensible" it becomes accessible as well as understandable.

Films that represent the past contribute to a culture's vision of itself, suggesting that the creation of public memory and a sense of national identity are intertwined. Recent writing on the impact of film on public memory has focused on how films that address the problem of memory foreground the past as a rhetorical arena. Public memory is, by definition, a site of conflicting discourses, "always contested and never neutral."[118] Identity itself becomes part of what is constructed in the process of assertion and opposition.

If memory is the process of recovering a sense of lived experience, the physical and emotional ephemera of historical figures provides essential material in the construction process. In examining several facets of the construction of national identity in American historical films of the 1990s, Robert Burgoyne recognizes what he terms "sensuous" ways of understanding history, strategies for gaining access to the literal "sense" of social memory as "the cultural desire to reexperience the past in a sensuous form [that] has become an important, perhaps decisive, factor in the struggle to lay claim to what and how the nation remembers."[119] Evoking lived experience allows access to the otherwise inaccessible. It asserts that the physical and emotional, what we customarily think of as a response to evidence, deserve consideration as evidence of history. Burgoyne adds that "in my view, the contemporary desire to reexperience history in a sensuous way speaks to an analogous desire to dispel the aura of the past as object of professional historical contemplation and to restore it to the realm of affective experience in a form that is comparable to sensual memory."[120]

The "sensuous" is that which we can feel; we use the adjective to describe something that is accessible to the senses. In order to recover the "sensible" dimensions of history, film will address necessarily the tactile, the visceral, and the affective elements of what it represents, through the visual and aural. In a discussion of the synaesthetic qualities of silent film,[121] for example, Melinda Szaloky details cognitive and phenomenological theories of how visual stimuli can evoke the experience of sound. While it is not addressed directly in this literature, I would like to suggest that for comparable reasons, visual images also convey tactile and visceral sensations: recall, for example, the close-up of the boot crushing the hand of the boy who has just been shot while trying to flee with his mother down the Odessa Steps in Eisenstein's *Battleship Potemkin* (1925). We also describe what we can "feel" in both physical and emotional terms, suggesting the close relationship of the "sensible" and sentiment, the thoughts, views, attitudes, and opinions we derive based on what we "feel." In her analysis of intercultural cinema, Laura Marks discusses extensively the means by which filmic images allow opportunities for "haptic" perceptions, so that "a viewer relates bodily"[122] to what the film represents. Here "representation is inextricable from embodiment" in the process of evoking embodied memories.[123]

History rendered in tactile terms on film often places its physical and emotional material in narrative contexts. It re-presents what occurred in the past now not only as what can be sensed but also as what is "sensible," that is, what can become coherent through the feelings it evokes.

A tendency toward a more tactile, visceral, "haptic" approach to the problems of public memory and national identity is evident in both film and television docudramas of the last decade. This analysis will center on two television miniseries about the Holocaust, *Uprising* (J. Avnet, 2001) and *Nuremberg* (Y. Simoneau, 2000), and in feature films detailing the involvement of American troops in combat in Vietnam (*We Were Soldiers*, R. Wallace, 2002) and Somalia (*Black Hawk Down*, R. Scott, 2001). Despite their differences in subject matter the works share similar strategies: the television miniseries focus emphatically—structurally—not on chronology or causality as a means to historical intelligibility, but instead on recovering primary emotional responses to the experience of the Holocaust. *Uprising* explains the revolt of the Jews trapped in the Warsaw ghetto through its docudramatization of the inhumanity that made resistance necessary. *Nuremberg* addresses the legal and moral complexity of its war trial subject matter through the emotional prism of its central sensibility, U.S. Supreme Court Justice Robert Jackson, the American chief prosecutor. Both works remind their primarily American, new millennium audiences of the emotional forces that led to the formation of the state of Israel and its subsequent self-defense policies. The American combat features target the physical as a means to allow access to the experience of armed conflict. The detailed re-creation of sacrifice in both films leads logically to ask, sacrifice for what? Both films allow a range of possible answers.

These films re-create sensation and sentiment to forward claims about how we should understand ourselves and remember profound events that have shaped our sense of who we are. The dramatic re-creation of actual people and events in docudrama leads inevitably to moral perspective. Consequently the foregrounding of the physical and emotional in these works raises basic questions about the ethics of docudramatic representation: do these stories and their respective media of distribution honor or exploit their subjects? Do they reduce the complex or do they make it accessible? My purpose here is not to take up one side or the other, but instead to suggest how the debate over the ethics of docudramatic adaptation arises because of the performative nature of these works. They function performatively because of the warranting strategies that characterize their advocacy. Advocacy itself invites counterargument. Each film performs the role of advocacy through its forum of presentation and the rhetorical strategies that structure its discourse of re-creation.

Uprising and Holocaust Docudrama

Recent writing has addressed extensively the problematics of Holocaust memory in documentary and narrative film.[124] As television miniseries, both *Uprising* and *Nuremberg* find unique approaches to their subject matter by emphasizing responses to the Holocaust as much, if not more than Holocaust events themselves. In the face of the vast body of work detailing the evidence and proceedings of the trials of Nazi leaders as war criminals,[125] *Nuremberg* gives narrative priority to the personal relationships between the central figures involved in those events. In *Uprising* the world of the Warsaw ghetto in the early 1940s both evokes and explains the helplessness of Jews facing Nazi annihilation and the resistance that arose in the face of it. The miniseries also reminds, indirectly, as a consequence of its airing in the weeks after September 11, 2001, of the politicization of helplessness in the circumstances, rationales, and repercussions revolving around the creation of the state of Israel and its subsequent actions and policies.

Uprising makes evident some of the basic strategies of miniseries docudrama, depending, however, on a feature-film-like emphasis on physical violence in its depiction of vulnerable people who become armed resisters. Violence to the body functions as a means to make the past present through sensation. As shown originally on television the work unfolds over two nights. In the first half, the narrative establishes causality, showing building oppression, the helplessness of most of the Jews living in Warsaw, and a resistance movement taking root. The second half shows the effects of both oppression and resistance, and is in many ways a conventional war film foregrounding the combat of a resistance movement. Molotov cocktails destroy tanks; stubborn resistance fighters outgun storm troopers and strip them of their weapons. True to feature film-like conventions, the film depends upon star casting[126] and detailed, authentic mise en scene to generate a realism convincing enough to authenticate its docudramatic re-creation.

Uprising, not surprisingly, bears strong similarities to *Schindler's List* (S. Spielberg, 1993) and *The Pianist* (R. Polanski, 2002). All re-create Polish Jewish ghetto life under the Nazi regime. As docudramas, these works draw on fundamental elements of melodrama in bringing moral perspective to their re-creation, including detailing the most repressive possible kind of social system, setting events within a hellish environment that makes resistance and escape necessary, and drawing upon a familial depiction of oppressed characters.[127] Any autonomous action within this context of institutionalized self-destruction becomes an act of resistance and is, consequently, morally mandated.

Eventually the Warsaw ghetto is reduced to a literal hell. Nothing remains of it but burning, smoking rubble, out of which emerges wraith-like souls who have survived the inferno. The last half of *Uprising* is extremely dark, lit almost entirely by fires, or torches in basements and sewers.

While the idea that the Nazis created hell on earth for the Jews they attempted to annihilate is not new, *Uprising* is unusual in two, interrelated respects: it tells a story of Jewish resistance, and shows graphically, as a television network movie-of-the-week, the violence that created that resistance. The film's re-creation of physical harm, its display of both action and resistance as reaction, establishes the moral system that defines resistance. Characters throughout the film bear wounds, the physical evidence of beatings. A brother convinces his sister, a ballet dancer, to have her leg broken, because they believe that the crippled will not be deported to a concentration camp. It is a world in which action, any action that supports survival, is the right thing to do.

A scene in which two musicians are beaten is pivotal in depicting the birth of resistance. The incident marks the end of accepting a world in which people will be brutalized without taking action. The Nazis have just broken up a recital in the ghetto's school and conservatory. They stop two violinists in the street and order the older to begin to play. As he complies one of the storm troopers circles him, and smashes him in the head with the butt of his rifle. He orders the younger musician still standing to begin to play.   The man begins a Strauss waltz, while the trooper begins the same, circling movement.   The two young men who will become the leaders of the Warsaw ghetto resistance movement have watched this unfold.   They approach, pull pistols, and shoot the soldiers, leaving the musician standing there, his colleague's blood spattered on his face and violin.

The graphic violence of the scene, unusual for a made-for-television film, addresses the need to access the brutality of this experience. The visceral nature of the images makes specific and personal, and thus tactile and tangible, the enormity of oppression and the terms of survival. The scene fuses passion for culture and its enduring values with the passionate necessity to resist oppression. Ultimately it indicates the death of classical culture and suggests what options are there to replace it.

The iconography of oppression and resistance in *Uprising* argues that if we can sense history, if it becomes physically and emotionally accessible, then we can make sense of it.   The foregrounding of the physical and emotional in this instance inevitably raises basic questions that grow out of both the ethics and politics of docudramatic representation.   Airing the series in the context of increasingly deteriorating political tensions in the mid-east after the fall of 2000 perhaps inadvertently illustrates a central paradox of recent Israeli politics. One function of the historical accuracy of the re-creation is that it valorizes the combative spirit of Zionism. The hellish irony of Nazi-forced self-destruction conceivably doubles back on itself.   As the miniseries argues for the necessity of Jewish survival, showing how decisive action breaks the cycle of forced self-destruction Polish Jews experienced in the Warsaw ghetto, it argues for identifying with a guerilla viewpoint by illustrating unjust occupation and the experience of the oppressed. Re-creating the Warsaw ghetto uprising evokes the analogy, to whatever extent it might be valid. My point is simply this: history emphasizing physical and emotional particulars becomes, in this instance, in every sense of the phrase, a two-edged sword.

And what are the ethical implications here? Does presenting this material as story through a commercial medium of distribution honor or exploit its subjects? Does it reduce the complex or make it accessible?[128]

The most fundamental issue remains representation itself. *Uprising* and similar docudramas not only present this subject matter, but as works of classic Hollywood narrative form, do so through the excess of the "body too many" of performers playing the roles of real-life principals.[129] This level of debate then hinges on the issue of whether or not the performance of victimization can serve the sanctity of memory in the same way as the constant reminder of absence—reminder without representation— that Elie Wiesel has advocated.[130]

When representation does occur the debate shifts levels, as it questions the usefulness and implications of representing the Holocaust in docudrama. Is any reminder of the Holocaust self-evidently worthwhile? Are such representations helpful? One line of argument arising recently has been that creating an awareness of traumatic history can be therapeutic. Do Holocaust representations create a form of therapeutic treatment of traumatic experience by evoking it as sensuous history? Or does docudramatic representation become problematic by numbing audiences to the experience and memory of the Holocaust? The potential for both outcomes exists within the form of docudrama. To see how, it makes sense first to consider what might be "traumatic" in the performance of traumatic events.

Docudramatic re-creation foregrounds the very performative nature of its representation. In the same sense that a speech act conveys assertive force because of the presence of the body of the speaker, docudramatic re-creation uses—depends upon—the force of performance. In speech the force of assertion stems from the presence of the body of the speaker, and the belief in the power that body's presence potentially represents.[131] Hate speech, for example, becomes problematic because the force—the potential damage—of its declarations threatens to exceed the "mere" exchange of ideas. The same issues pertain to docudrama as it argues for a definition of history through the performative force of re-creation. If the performance of the physical and emotional make it accessible, what is the effect of the assertive force of its performance? It is useful to return briefly to Joshua Hirsch's suggestion that "posttraumatic cinema" evokes the traumatic experience but does so in a context that works to "make sense" of it,[132] not through the neat conventions and containments of traditional, historical narrative, but instead through the disruptions of a self-conscious narrative. The kind of cinema that will contribute constructively to the post-traumatic historical consciousness Hirsch is describing acknowledges its inability to control the performance of the past. "Insofar as posttraumatic narration is a kind of failure of narration–a collapse of mastery over time and point of view—it, too, tends toward a self-conscious voice, toward a consideration of its own failure to master the past."[133]   Hirsch sees the temporal structures of a documentary such as *Night and Fog* as both evoking a posttraumatic consciousness and as movement toward such an acknowledgment.

For their part docudramas tend to adhere to the conventional, classical Hollywood narrative characteristics of historical film in general, however, their very performativity creates the potential for such an acknowledgment. The "body too many" that is characteristic of docudramatic re-creation signposts performance per se. Docudramatic re-creation offers double performatives. It acknowledges its failure to "master" the past in its self-evident strategizing. Star casting and feature film packaging give its absent referents a presence.

Star casting gives equal weight to performer and performance. Casting in *Uprising* serves to illustrate how the performative dimensions of the work highlight the positions of this debate. Casting David Schwimmer as Yitzhak Zuckerman foregrounds how the docudramatic re-creation of an historic person consists of multiple superimposed texts. In fall, 2001 Schwimmer had performed most notably as Ross in the CBS situation comedy *Friends* as well as Captain Herbert Sobel in the concurrently released HBO miniseries, *Band of Brothers*. Star casting here arguably provides as much the compression effect of Hollywood conventions—a sign of the control and containment of the history that this particular "Zuckerman" signifies—as a self-conscious acknowledgment of the mechanism of that process. We find docudrama narrating and simultaneously signposting the terms of its narration.

Schwimmer's performance, much like the splattered blood that evokes simultaneously the Nazis' action against the Warsaw ghetto gymnasium and the continuing annihilation by the Nazis of the history of civilized thought, behavior, and values in Eastern Europe, exemplify the excess of docudramatic re-creation. Accordingly we are offered a sensuous history, a representation of the past that argues through presence, rather than sacred absence. It is that very excess that purports to recover the literally unrepresentable, the physical and emotional material of the past, and consequently creates competing views of its utility: is it distracting substitution, or is it self-conscious signposting of its own terms of representation?   That the debate surrounding performative forms of representation arises at all tells us that it does what history needs to do: it not only reminds, but also makes us aware that our efforts to remember will always be a result of how and why we construct the past.

Nuremberg

Yves Simoneau's *Nuremberg* (2000) devotes its narrative energy to developing a coherent sense of the how the principal figures involved responded to the events surrounding the Nuremberg war trials. In adapting its historical subject matter the miniseries does the work of docudrama in the most literal sense: it dramatizes documents, so that the interaction of documentary material in a docudramatic context is itself performative.

As docudrama, the miniseries enters and references a series of adaptations, including Joseph E. Persico's book with its own formulation of primary and secondary materials, reportage of the original events (news and trial transcripts), and previous films, plays, and the precedents for presentation that they establish. This particular *Nuremberg* approaches its subject with less concern for history (although it does provide occasional chronological indicators) or legality (it also offers equally fragmentary explanations of legal issues and the procedures involved) than some of its precedents.[134] Simoneau's adaptation purports to re-create the personal experience of the trials through a web of relationships built around two focal points, American prosecutor and Supreme Court Justice Robert Jackson (Alec Baldwin), and the trial's number one defendant, Reichmarschall Hermann Goering (Brian Cox). The film uses this web to personalize legal and moral issues.

The central issue affecting these relationships is the meaning of the trials. For Jackson, the trial of key Nazi leaders as war criminals provides a necessary opportunity to define their actions and policies as the criminal acts of criminal conspirators. Consequent punishment would then be justified in a legal as well as a moral sense. Goering, his antagonist, argues that the trial is nothing more meaningful than role play.

While the trial presents Jackson with a professional and moral challenge, it offers Goering a last opportunity to perform. The former head of the Luftwaffe is characterized from the moment of his surrender as a performer, a storyteller capable of charming immediately even his American army captors. Goering is larger physically than any of the other defendants; he dresses differently, wearing pieces of his old uniforms and his trademark dark aviator sunglasses during the trial. He conveys an attitude of untouchability in what he does and says. He views everything from the routine of their incarceration to the translation headphones they wear during the trial as a joke. Throughout he urges his codefendants to dismiss the meaning of their trial and confinement. They are not criminals, he argues, but are merely the vanquished.

As his case gets underway Jackson is criticized for his "stultifying" documentary approach to the prosecution. The trial, he is warned, is "a show." The film suggests that the prosecution risks losing the trial for an additional reason: by definition, as a trial, the procedure gives defendants, Goering in particular, the opportunity to testify. Testifying creates a forum for them, an opportunity to express a wide range of opinions, views, and philosophical positions beyond the points the defendants have been asked to testify about. In essence, *Nuremberg* argues Jackson's basic problem is that Goering is a superior performer. The narrative structure of the miniseries suggests that the turning point in the clash between Jackson and Goering occurs when the prosecution places into evidence film of the concentration camps.

The images from the U. S. Army's *Nazi Concentration Camps* that unroll on the courtroom screen are documents that are now, of course, well known. The footage functions in *Nuremberg* in several ways. The screening is literally momentous, re-creating the experience of one of the first public audiences to see these images. Despite Jackson's problematic "documentary" strategy the film's actual photographic material cannot be upstaged by any performance, neither by any individual defendant's, nor by its narrative purpose as it is incorporated within a made-for-television docudrama.

The documentary footage assumes additional rhetorical functions when it appears in the context of a movie-of-the-week docudrama. The interaction created by the placement of indexical images on a screen in a re-created courtroom argues for the proximity to, and the authority of the re-creation and the actual events it references. While the footage itself provides the necessary data, the visible evidence to swing momentum to the prosecution, it also warrants the particular claims about the priority of response to events this docudramatic adaptation favors, and does so performatively.

As it displays an actual documentary film within a narrative re-creation the scene gives equal visual weight to both screen and the audience within the scene. We who know this material are accordingly positioned to watch and listen to the on-screen audience watching it for the first time. The structure of the scene indicates how the film's evidence legitimizes the responses of the court, the on-screen spectators, and by implication, those of us in the audience for the miniseries.[135] The film re-creates these responses emphatically through aural cues, the gasps and sobs on the sound track, through cut-aways to individual reactions of judges, prosecutors, defendants, and courtroom spectators, and by long shot views of the courtroom. These show the film on the screen in the background, and people, ostensibly overwhelmed by what they are seeing on the screen, standing and leaving while the film continues to roll. These exits are punctuated by the judges themselves standing to leave after the film has concluded.

The documentary functions performatively as it fulfills the role, the purpose, of the warrant the argument requires. It stands alone, yet it also interacts with its re-created context, and in doing so provides a basis to reason from evidence to claims regarding the import, the historical materiality, of emotional response. The re-creation of emotional and physical responses to the evidence mandates the moral argument Jackson has been advocating. The scene allows the documentary footage to fulfill a role beyond its primary function. It offers not only data, but also further warrants the claims of the docudrama about the importance of recovering and regarding as the substance of history the original emotional responses to the events of the trial. Recovering emotion, the scene suggests, is as material to the moment as the screening's impact on memory (its record of what happened) and identity (its definition of those involved).

Nuremberg's incorporation of documentary material throws into relief the interlacing systems and associated codes that constitute the adaptation. The miniseries depends upon its rhetorical structures, its documentary data, served through emotional warrants, to forward its moral claims. The rhetorical thrust of the film is possible only because of the merger of documentary material, historical framework, narrative presentational structure, and the melodramatic codes put into play by docudramatic representation. The rhetorical appeal of *Nuremberg* derives from its performative qualities: its modeling of known figures, actions, and events; its interlacing of re-created material modeled on actuality, and the documentary imagery it interacted with; and its larger formulation as television miniseries, replete with its fusion of classic Hollywood narrative and melodramatic modes of representation.

Black Hawk Down and *We Were Soldiers*

These recent war docudramas target the physical as a means to allow access to the emotional experience of war, and accordingly, the meaning that experience allows. Although they represent different wars, *Black Hawk* and *Soldiers* both argue for the retrieval of a sense of identity through a sensuous, visceral history. The films define and specifically visualize identity as the sacrifice of one's body that service in the United

States armed forces demands. In this sense they are precursors to Katherine Bigelow's war docudramas, *K-19: The Widowmaker* (2002) and the more fictionalized *The Hurt Locker* (2008). In both of Bigelow's films the "work" of men in service requires nothing less than hands-on contact with explosive forces. The protective suits the work requires in both her films only serves to call attention to the devastating impact of warfare on the individual human body   *Black Hawk* and *Soldiers*, like both the Bigelow films, are "rescue" stories; despite the difference in time, setting, and issues at conflict, the individuals whose stories we see in *Black Hawk* and *Soldiers* are "rescued" not simply from desperate, life-threatening combat situations, but also from contentious national policies.

Black Hawk and *Soldiers* re-create events to provide necessary data, and use the re-creation of physical damage to actual individuals to warrant their larger arguments about national policy and national identity. As Americans we are, the films would argue, both our mistakes and our efforts to correct them.

Black Hawk and *Soldiers* extend the traditional iconography of the combat film to re-create their visions of armed service, and the particular physicality, the viscerality, of the wars they depict. Certainly war films have always suggested, if not shown explicitly, the damage war inflicts upon the human body. Since *Saving Private Ryan* (S. Spielberg, 1998) the war film has drawn upon digital sound and image technologies that make it possible to depict combat's carnage with unprecedented graphic specificity. The horrors *Black Hawk* and *Soldiers* recover stems not only from what we see and hear, but also from the basis of these images in actuality. The graphic depictions in these films are filmic re-creations of particular, actual events, most recounted in detail and faithfully adapted from the accounts of these events in prior, written sources.[136] The rigorous detailing of damage to the bodies of American soldiers in both prose and filmic accounts serves to prod a larger, cultural memory of these events, and from this to allow these stories to contribute to a sense of national identity at a time when physically, culturally, and symbolically, the United States has been attacked and attacked in return.

In the mode of the traditional combat film, both *Black Hawk* and *Soldiers* define "service" as the courageous actions of American combatants and their leaders, and center on that action as the first layer of their visual surfaces. *Soldiers* details the first large-scale conflict American troops faced in Vietnam's Ia Drang River valley in November, 1965. *Black Hawk* explains events nearly thirty years later surrounding the loss of dozens of American soldiers in Somalia in October, 1993. In both films American combat units are surrounded, facing overwhelming odds as a numerically superior enemy launches relentless attacks on its own terrain, the mountains and jungles of Vietnam, and the walls and streets of the city of Mogadishu. The service the American soldiers render is stalwart. Leaders and followers never falter. Mel Gibson's Colonel Hal Moore in *Soldiers* strongly suggests John Wayne's solid, physical presence, stalking leadership decisions as the battle opens up in the Vietnamese jungle around him.[137]

"Service" in these films means quite literally to see the results when American troops put their bodies on the line. Both films emphasize the physical, visceral nature of the action and events they show, concentrating on wounds, mounds of bodies, and damage to vehicles. Both cover visual imagery with an equally horrific sound environment. The action in *Soldiers* often consists of shot after shot of soldiers wounded in every conceivable part of the human anatomy, re-creating Moore's own descriptive prose in his book that the film adapts. Thumbs, fingers, hands, arms, legs, heads, necks, torsos, groins, etc. are all grist for the mill here.[138] In following Bowden's book *Black Hawk* singles out notable incidents: one soldier is struck by a rocket-propelled grenade that does not explode but remains sticking out of his chest; another soldier is blown in half, his half-torso dragged out of the front of the Humvee in which he had been sitting. Wounded men remain alive and conversant, underlining further along with the visual evidence the implications of damage to the body. Combat culminates in heaps of dead bodies, in a soccer stadium in Mogadishu, and at Landing Zone X-Ray the troops have been defending in the Ia Drang valley. Modes of transportation such as jeeps and helicopters assume an almost personal resonance because they provide extensions of the human body. In *Black Hawk* the helicopters that are at the center of the story are shot down, shot up, but are not nearly as bullet-riddled as the Humvees carrying the troops through the city streets. *Soldiers* shows its Hueys becoming full of the same kind of bullet holes as they bring men and supplies into the landing zone, and leave with the wounded and the dead. The visible damage to jeeps and helicopters provides yet another index of the physical reality of battle. Vehicles appear awash with blood. As post-*Saving Private Ryan* combat films both have surround-sound pinging, zinging bits of bullets and shrapnel to amplify the horror and helplessness of immersion in a firefight. The emphasis on physical damage suggests stigmata, visible evidence of the sacrifice necessary in the cause of service. The ideology that demands sacrifice becomes more evidently the cross we bear as Americans.

Both *Black Hawk* and *Soldiers* are rescue stories.[139] Trapped, stranded patrols must be brought back, dead or alive. The solemn mission in both is that no soldier will be left behind. The physical evidence the films re-create emphasizes the cost of such a mission. Within the traditional combat iconography that details these events the core narrative conflict then suggests that whether it is Vietnam or Eastern Africa, we need to rescue ourselves from policies that put our troops at risk. Further, rescue is necessary to our sense of identity. In essence, our sense of who we are as a country is what we end up needing to rescue here. It is perhaps the strongest element of post-September 11 exigence that emerges from these two films.[140]

The depiction of "service" in these films leads immediately to questions of policy. They are films that praise service while at the same time indicating the error of waging war as an instrument of flawed policy.[141] To show these events leads logically to asking, why did they occur in the first place? Why was the courage and self-sacrifice the films depict necessary? *Black Hawk* confronts this question directly.   At the conclusion of the film a statement appears on screen faulting the Clinton administration policy that allowed this to happen, and to happen this way. *Soldiers* (both as a book and as a film) never addresses the "big" question of why these soldiers were dropped into this landing zone, in this particular river valley. In the film adaptation their mission to "engage the enemy" is never clarified in the context of either a defensive or offensive strategy, and thereby adapts faithfully the basic American perspective toward the war in Vietnam in general, and certainly in 1965 in particular.[142] Both films show American troops being attacked. The irony is that it is only by implication that we understand that they are attackers who are being attacked. The bulk of the action appears to be self-defense rather than aggression. Ultimately any sense of who these wars might help is not the issue the films work out. The films define what it means to be American through the acts of rescuing American soldiers whose survival is at risk. The moral perspective *Soldiers* and *Black Hawk* allows highlights, on the one hand, the honor, the professionalism, and the nobility of the American soldier.   That same perspective, growing out of the very viscerality of the films as historical records, also compels asking what their sacrifices have been for.

The films' arguments about American identity create ambivalence. While paying tribute to the combatants they portray, both films make it possible to raise questions about combat as a policy (and the policies that create combat). These are feature film docudramas. Is an entertainment venue an effective opportunity to raise questions about policy and the reality of its repercussions? Does the value of remembrance (of sacrifice) counterbalance the ethical implications of framing self-sacrifice as entertainment, and of depicting that sacrifice in images of bodily exposure, penetration, and destruction? The graphic specificity of these films can only represent and approximate the experience of combat. Can "entertainment" allow the intellectual engagement with the issues these representations raise and deserve? If they do lead to some greater understanding, will that in turn have meaning? Will it lead to avoidance, elimination, or perhaps some kind of more effective waging of war? *Black Hawk* splits its view of combat, placing us among the men on the ground, and by contrast, cutting away frequently to video monitors in the operation command centers showing distant, sanitized, aerial views of the carnage. The film's visual structure here suggests that the leaders of the men being shredded below relate to the action as viewers of a TV show. Through these films do we really understand our own natures better, or are we collaborating within and helping perpetuate the same unreal, "game" thinking that culturally reinforces the values that perpetuate war—that take us away from it, that abstract, and that market war as an entertainment product? Despite their graphic specificity and their bases in actuality, are these films that argue that for key decision-makers, war will always be just a game?

Some Implications of "Feeling" History

These films would remedy the possibility that an important part of history, the sensations and feelings that significant events arouse, is fleeting, difficult to access, to record, and is easily relegated to a realm of implication. After conventional history addresses chronology, causes, problems, and the action of events, it leaves up to inference the passions and sensations that also occurred. The docudramatic mode of representation becomes a logical means of recovering the physical sensations and emotions that are arguably important keys to understanding our past. Consequently *Black Hawk* and *Soldiers* develop for us the horror and entrapment that characterize American combat experience in Vietnam and Somalia. These same films also highlight some implications of their presentation as docudrama. In arguing for what should be remembered, and how memory will shape our sense of who we are, their re-creations package some of the most profound experiences of our past in products that are mediated for profit. Their narratives arguably impose simplistic formal and moral perspectives on the inherently complex and irreducible material of extreme human experience. Their feature film packaging may undercut even the most graphically specific depiction of the reality of the damage that war causes. Equally implicit, however, is the recognition that in recovering the personal, the physical, and emotional, that these films are tributes, that their re-creation honors, rather than exploits their real-life principals.[143] Accordingly, they present the morally complex in terms that are accessible because the physical and emotional have been framed by the moral issues raised by defining identity. Feature film presentation, star casting, and the production values that make physical and emotional experience visual and therefore accessible signpost the docudramatic mode of representation. Docudrama announces itself, and so proclaims the status of its material, its strategies of representation, and the proximity of its re-creation to its referents. The strategies of modeling the real, of allowing the real and its re-creation to follow from and mix with each other frame the performative nature of docudrama and underline the indexically iconic nature of its representation.

CHAPTER ELEVEN

"MOVIE-OF-THE-WEEK" DOCUDRAMA, "HISTORICAL-EVENT" TELEVISION AND THE STEVEN SPIELBERG MINISERIES *BAND OF BROTHERS*

DEREK PAGET AND STEVEN N. LIPKIN

Introduction

As researchers of film and television docudrama for many years, we were drawn to the Steven Spielberg/Tom Hanks miniseries *Band of Brothers* for a number of reasons.[144] Docudrama's attempted fusion of the factual and the fictional makes it, perhaps, the most challenging of the hybrid forms introduced into dramatic representation by television. Over the sixty-odd years of its television history it has been most challenging in terms of the demand it makes of audiences (to distinguish between that which can be shown to have happened, and that which can be imagined to have happened). The justifying rubrics of television docudrama tend to oscillate between its "host" genres documentary and drama in ways that keep it a fresh though occasional element in television scheduling. Its impact on movie making, too, has been impressive (especially as film and television industries have converged).

We are both also fascinated by the tendency over several generations for film and television drama to reach again and again for stories drawn from the "Good War," as World War Two is sometimes known. We would argue that modern Anglo-American culture and society has been profoundly shaped by such stories in terms of its ethics and values, and its politics. There is a post-Good War side to the making of war docudrama that is potentially much darker, with stories of war told in order to justify and explain foreign policy interventions in new conjunctures. The war sub-genre of docudrama has provided apparently limitless opportunities for reflections of, and interventions in, past and current geopolitical debate.

Stories of war have also presented opportunities for docudrama to be taken seriously, something not always easily achieved given the genre's "Movie-of-the-Week" background. Although we have both argued for the genre's right to be considered, at its best, a central one in the history of modern media, dismissal of docudrama is still relatively regular. It is "disease-of-the-week" television, we are told—an afternoon panacea for the anxious in society (a "woman's genre" some sexist commentary would have it). It is untrustworthy, conflating as it does genres that are, properly considered, opposites. "How true are the facts?" is always prominent in the FAQs about docudrama we find ourselves being asked by non-academic friends and acquaintances. The form is often seen as having a tendency towards cheapness and simplification: low budget /"low concept."[145]

By contrast, *Band of Brothers* is a series made at the very top end of the "high concept" budgetary scale, by talented and internationally famous *film* personnel for a cutting edge cable TV network (Home Box Office) and the most venerable and prestigious of national television institutions (the BBC). Its high status, its war story, its basis in fact, its mix of British and American actors and makers, its location in the medium of television, and its aim at international markets—all make it a fascinating case study for the scholarly act of interpretation.

Band of Brothers—An Elegy and a Memorial

This ten-part miniseries, premiered in late 2001, adapted historian Stephen Ambrose's eponymous (and popular) 1992 book about World War Two unit "Easy Company" of the U.S. Army's 506th Regiment, 101st Airborne Division. The company's story from formation, through D-Day, to the final acts of the war was timely in a double sense. On the one hand, it coincided with historical anniversaries of World War Two events that had been unfolding in the media throughout the 1990s; on the other, it resonated with more recent American and "allied" military interventions and their consequences. These latter had been consistently represented in feature film through the kinds of *rhetoric* (and we use the word deliberately) associated especially with World War Two. Elements of these rhetorics can be found both in *Band of Brothers* and in the collaboration between Ambrose, Spielberg and Hanks that preceded it, the feature film *Saving Private Ryan* (1998).

In the movement towards oral history that runs behind many recent representations of World War Two lurks a dawning realization: battlefield survivors of "The Good War" will not be with us for ever. Ken Burns's documentary series *The War* showed the keenness with which this fact is now felt. It was screened to (for documentary) astonishingly large TV audiences on American PBS in 2007. In pre-publicity Burns pointed out that a thousand veterans were dying every day. Soon, the witnesses will all be gone, as have their forbears from the Great War.[146]

The World War Two "Private Ryan generation" is dying out in other combatant countries too, and the metaphor of their experience cuts across national boundaries in part because of prior representation in the arts. Thus the tone of *Ryan* and *Band* is an almost poetic one of *elegy*; Ambrose's source book, too, has this valedictory tone.[147] Works of popular history based on—even consisting mainly of—testimony have proliferated in recent years. In 1998, close to the fiftieth anniversary of the war's end, NBC news anchor Tom Brokaw published *The Greatest Generation* and he has compiled other testimony histories following the success of that book. Britain's Lyn Macdonald began to publish testimony histories about World War 1 in the 1980s. In many ways all these writers are in debt to Studs Terkel's pioneering works of oral history which include, of course, his 1984 book about the Ryan generation, *The Good War*. "Historical event history," linked to oral testimony, has influenced docudrama profoundly.[148]

Band of Brothers was inspired directly by an oral history encounter, Ambrose taking on the project as a result of a group interview he conducted with Easy Company veterans in 1988. Ambrose says: "As they talked about other members of the company, about various reunions over the decades, it became obvious that they continued to be a band of brothers."[149]

His response to these men could not be clearer—it operated on a human, we might even say on a "manly," level rather than an academic one. It was not, we would argue, entirely the response of the profession in which he had spent his life. The tone of the "professoriat," as Robert Rosenstone calls historian colleagues[150] is largely absent from Ambrose's book. But it has, perhaps, been all the more attractive to a popular, non-historian readership—and to filmmakers—as a result. Academic historians, often suspicious of popular history, can be doubly suspicious of history conveyed by popular film. But recent academic theory in the study of history has actively acknowledged the potential of narrative to deliver *considered* (if somewhat unacademic) popular history. The constructed nature of all discourse applies fully as much to the writing of academic history as to any other representational mode.[151] In offering something different, in parting company with the language of the professoriat, Ambrose himself can be seen as a kind of hybrid. Like the docudrama inspired by his book, he offers insight into character and situation as well as the abstract forces of history. These are gifts more usually associated with a novelist. His collaborator Douglas Brinkley made this explicit in a valedictory tribute to Ambrose:

> Wherever Steve went, crowds of veterans would mob him. They called him the *poet laureate* of World War II. He was a *genius storyteller* with a gift for making the past come alive.[152]

In Spielberg, Ambrose found a filmmaker collaborator also gifted in storytelling. As *Guardian* journalist Rupert Smith remarked, *Ryan* "set new standards for war films, and...set the seal on the American pre-eminence in the field."[153] In making *Band of Brothers*, Spielberg/Hanks were able to capitalize—literally and metaphorically—on the success of *Saving Private Ryan* and also to extend its reach through the potential a "long form" TV series has to develop a larger narrative canvas with a wider group of characters. It is important that this television series was made in the more prestigious medium of *film*, however. *Band*'s status as film connects it to another history and tradition, one with a higher cultural currency than that of television. Utilizing afresh some of the characteristic tropes of the Hollywood War Movie, Spielberg/Hanks expanded *Ryan*'s evocation of the D-Day landings and 1944-45 combat in France and Germany in ways made possible by the durational factors of a miniseries.

First, however, we would draw attention to two stylistic aspects of *Band of Brothers* that the series shares with the feature film *Saving Private Ryan*:

1] Classic Hollywood war film structuring.

Despite its unusual ten episode structure, *Band* initially represents a return to the familiar iconography of the World War Two combat film. Its combat unit is socially and geographically diverse enough to suggest a cross-section of American society. Plots organized around the culturally and morally *representative group* are common in war movie history. The group has so often been a platoon that Oliver Stone eventually made a 1986 film with that single word title. The platoon as the *part*, metonymic of an army *whole*, facilitates narrative arcs associated with representative acts of cowardice and bravery, desperation and fortitude that can be focused on individuals with whom audiences can empathize and from whose experience they are invited to generalize. So concentrated was Stone's use of the platoon metonym that his two sergeant characters were almost literal embodiments of abstract "Good" and "Evil" the like of which has not been seen since medieval European liturgical drama.

By contrast, the *Band of Brothers* "long form" was focused on a *company*, with a commensurate increase in the number of characters. In this expanded metonym, individual characters do not bear as much signifying weight as they tend to do in feature film. Here characters function much more within the unifying concept of *brotherhood*. Hence each episode focuses on different character sets, with the character of Richard Winters (Damian Lewis) not so much functioning as sole protagonist, more as signifier of the company's continuing brotherhood. Apart from him and one or two others, the essential sameness of appearance of soldiers (when seen in such numbers across ten episodes) made it hard to identify with individuals, easier to respond to the idea that the company was the unifying collective principle. This was very much a feature of Ambrose's source text—to some extent characters come and go, as it were, but the *company* remains.

Audiences familiar with Spielberg's re-creation of D-Day in *Ryan*, audiences intertextually aware of the tropes of other war films, could find much to relate to in *Band*. The cinematic past inhabits the series as fully as the historical past. Something similar animated *Saving Private Ryan* for, as Nigel Morris has pointed out in his 2007 book Spielberg is a director whose works are frequently self-reflexive, functioning as a kind of personal commentary on cinema history. *Band*'s trope of the combat unit refers *back* in that "Easy Company" is the archetypal and familiar representative combat unit, its members' chancy survival or death setting up the major concerns of each episode of the series. But the format also allowed the filmmakers to develop a more nuanced view of the collective in warfare.

2] Actuality images.

Some of the development in actuality footage and still images since World War Two has been technological (more portability in combat for camera and microphone). Some has been social and cultural (we think here of issues of access—those signalled by jargon words such as "embedded," for example). Images of World War Two are by contrast less problematic than current images because over time they have achieved iconic status. The photographs of Robert Capa and newsreel footage such as the concentration camps material shown at the Nuremberg Trials are examples of this authority. The new potential for immediacy has also been problematized by digital technology's ability to play off—and play with—the fictional and the factual (mixing actuality with, for example, digitally manipulated footage). Modern representations of warfare in docudrama thus fuse the "Then" and the "Now," as evidenced in both *Ryan* and *Band*. Their "saturated, flared and chaotic" look and style builds on the Capa-look (in his D-Day photographs, for example) and contributes a quasi-documentary power to the dramatic narrative.[154] To coin a phrase, the "Then-ness of Then" is posed within the sequence against the "Now-ness of Now" in ways that only analysis of the work as *docudrama* can fully reveal.[155]

The American Context

Band of Brothers must first be seen as a docudrama made in America within an American context, transmitted in the year of, at very time of, the events that have come to be symbolized by the numbers "9/11." This made reception in America of a different order to reception elsewhere. Even though its story is firmly located in the history of the 1940s, the arguments *Band* makes about the leadership necessary for this group to survive ultimately roots the Easy Company saga squarely in the experience of a 2001 audience. Especially true for America, this posed related questions for other audiences. During the Clinton administration the American public viewed with something like approval the controlled effectiveness of its military in Bosnia in the face of a Holocaust-like ethnic cleansing. The debacle in Somalia in 1993 underlined a new context in which the impotence of the American army in certain situations of modern warfare was highlighted by images of the corpse of an American GI being dragged through the streets of Mogadishu.[156] The September 11 terrorist attacks reactivated a Pearl Harbor mindset in the United States; not surprisingly then, traditional war docudrama fits appropriately the culture of conflict subsequently encouraged by the Bush administration and its allies. In Europe, the reaction to the historical event was more equivocal, but still engaged.

Framed by the post-September 11 cultural context in, and outside, America, *Band* argues for strong, enabling leadership, and for the nobility of a war that is necessary to rescue Americans and American interests against a malign and alien ideology easily characterized as fanatical. Throughout, *Band* emphasizes the need for strong, effective leadership, beginning with issues raised in boot camp by the conflicts between a martinet officer, Captain Sobel (David Schwimmer), and his more naturally authoritative (and more efficient) subordinate Lieutenant Winters. Decisions made in each major campaign Easy Company faces amplify the debate about leadership at micro-(company) and macro-(army) levels.[157] The survival of the company depends indirectly on macro-decision making by its upper echelon leaders, but more importantly and dramatically on the strong leadership *on the ground* of men such as Winters. Ultimately, the clinching argument for leadership rests upon the persistence at company level of an army (and of the society behind that army) prepared to assert that profound wrongs can be, must be, resolved by the most powerful, effective military action possible. Even if the grand strategists get it wrong, the series suggests, Good Men can still prevail through shared values.

Band's appropriateness for its audience becomes understandable because of what Lipkin (2002) has identified as docudrama's "promotable, rootable, and relatable" functions.[158] The distant history of D-Day becomes relatable to a post-September 11 U. S. audience's need for effective leadership and rescue in an atmosphere of victimization. Promotion of the series before and concurrent with its premiere in November 2001 on HBO emphasized understandably the Spielberg/Hanks collaboration over similar D-Day subject matter in *Saving Private Ryan*.[159] Promotion for *Band* also created opportunities to carry public service announcements advocating support for creation of a World War Two veterans' memorial, noting once again that each day meant the passing of veterans. *Band* was promoted not simply as a television program, but as part of a necessary cultural event recognizing what was just and honorable in the United States' involvement in World War Two. In Britain, too, the series could be—and was—linked into programming associated with the upcoming Armistice Day, and with the very British concept of *remembrance*.[160]

That war is necessary is a governing premise here; each episode asserts specifically that, in light of this premise, the action we see is both necessary and ennobling. In tropes very familiar to movie-of-the-week docudrama, virtually each episode of *Band* is rooted in the problem of victims and the need for rescue. In the first episode the company as a whole turns to Winters and its sergeants to be rescued from the sadistic training strategies and incipient battlefield incompetence of Sobel. In the next episode Winters again provides the leadership that rescues two of Easy's platoons from the German defenders of heavy artillery emplacements near Utah Beach in Normandy. In the third episode, "Bull" Randleman (Michael Cudlitz), one of the more popular men in the company, temporarily goes missing and must be found, and the entire group must be rescued from attacking Panzers by the timely arrival of Sherman tanks. Episode four of the series has Easy Company rescuing the populace in a Dutch town; in five, Winters must be rescued from his own guilt; in six, Gene Roe (Shane Taylor) the company's medic is featured, rescuing a variety of wounded men; in seven, the company must again be

rescued from Lieutenant Dike (Peter O'Meara) and his incompetent
leadership; in eight, the second platoon is rescued by Winters from one
last, potentially disastrous night patrol. Conflict itself becomes the trial
these potential victims must endure—the trial that will ultimately make
Good Men of them, and reposition them not simply as victims but as
witnesses. These features will become more evident in a close analysis of
the final two episodes of the series.

Witnessing, Surviving and Testifying

The last two episodes of *Band of Brothers* illustrate how the series
argues for the interrelationship of bearing witness and the notion of rescue.
Part 9, "Why We Fight," begins and ends with Easy Company's
occupation of a small German town near the war's end in mid-April,
1945.[161] Part 10 follows the group from there to Berchtesgaden and the
taking of Hitler's Bavarian mountain retreat, the Eagle's Nest. Through
these concluding chapters the act of witnessing reveals two basic truths
about what has fuelled the war: in liberating a concentration camp near the
village of Landsberg, Easy Company bears witness to the profound evil
inherent in the policies of the Third Reich. By complete contrast, through
the breathtaking beauty and peace they find subsequently in the mountains
they are allowed to see the illegitimacy of the ideology that has presumed
that exercise of power has been its natural destiny. With both of these
revelations, the GIs' role as witnesses begins the redemption of place, the
reclaiming of what Germany must come to mean *now* through the Allied
victory. We understand the importance of witnessing in both episodes
because it is made momentous. In both, the act of bearing witness and its
implications follow a similar pattern. The moment, the process of
witnessing itself, assumes a magnitude through cinematic markers of the
scale of the experience. In both, a large part of what the act of bearing
witness registers is the absent presence of the vanquished foe. After all the
combat Easy Company has seen since D-Day, it is absence that now
indicates the nature of the evil they have faced. In both episodes, the act of
bearing witness is repeated and emphasized, reinforcing what it registers.
Finally, as with the rest of the series, the interviews with the real-life
principals that frame both episodes ties "Then" to "Now" indexically,
reiterating the import of lived history, warranting the larger arguments the
presence of survivor-witnesses forwards.

The performance of witnessing in docudrama provides a bridge between
past and present. The witness, it must be remembered, is a presence in
place as well as time. Witnesses embody the stamp of both time and place

as they represent through their testimony the events they have experienced. The moments of witness in these last two episodes of the series foreground cinematically the process of witnessing and the magnitude of what witnesses see. In Part 9, "Why We Fight," an Easy Company patrol is sent from the village to check the surrounding woods. We share their viewpoint. At first, we travel alongside the GIs as they stroll. As they become progressively more attuned to the quiet of the woods, they slow and begin scanning the tree branches above for snipers. Perspective shifts from above back to the side of the men. They advance in a line, and a few tendrils of smoke waft by their heads. The shot shifts again to show the entire group of men stopped at the edge of the tree line, staring straight ahead fixedly, directly at the point of the camera position. Both the pause in action and the shot of the group staring at the camera create the expectation of point of view, however the reverse angle that would complete the logic of the sequence is delayed. Whatever is there to see creates urgency. The close-up instead shows the running boots of one of the men as he returns to the village to bring the company's officers, Winters, Nixon (Ron Livingston), and Speirs (Matthew Settle). Subsequently it is their arrival at the same point in the woods we see next, and again what we see is them confronting whatever it is that is there to be witnessed.

The reiterated point of view structure and the delay in completing its sequence of shots foreground the importance of the moment of witness. When we are allowed to see what has given the entire group pause—the gates and fence of the concentration camp with its emaciated survivors staring back—the moment has been made "momentous." Awareness of the magnitude of what they are seeing grows slowly in all the men, however Winters and Nixon become our main reference points. The horror of the camp—the gaunt, damaged state of the survivors, the piles of burning bodies creating the smoke that attracted the attention of the patrol, the slow but continuing emergence of walking skeletons from tiny barracks stacked with the living and dead—becomes registered in the scene through the insistent return to point of view. As Winters begins to walk forward slowly, trying to absorb what he sees, the camera tracks around and with him, alternately showing him, and showing what he confronts. Nixon witnesses the camp the same way. Incorporating the moving camera into the traditional point of view structure of the moment underlines the impact of witnessing on each man. Shots of each man in the company reacting to the scene further multiply its magnitude.

The point of view structures in the scene—the connection of place and witness—frame the markings of damage. Shots of witnesses and the reverse angle representations of what they see equates the physical harm done here to bodies—starvation, wounds, death, and the desecration of the dead—as indicators of the evil responsible. Germany's darkest secret is metonymically uncovered in this place and others like it. By contrast, point of view strategies in Part 10 serve to foreground the very magnitude and majesty of space itself. When Easy Company arrives at the peak crowned by the Eagle's Nest, the scene favors very long shots, shown mostly from a third person, rather than subjective perspective, to display the idyllic beauty of snowcapped Alps, mountain lakes, and sunlight streaming through trees. The shots echo intertextually Hitler's own home movies. The episode begins with a high angle long shot tracking with Winters as he walks through the sunlit woods to the edge of the mountain lake, dressed now not in fatigues but a bathing suit. If bearing witness in the previous episode was horrific, what the men of Easy Company find here allows them a well-deserved sense of peace.

A key link between the horror of the concentration camp and the beauty of Hitler's mountain retreat is the remaining traces of an absent enemy. At the camp one of the survivors reveals that the guards had left only that morning. They ran out of bullets to shoot the remaining inmates. The visible evidence of their actions, however, remains all around. Similarly in the Eagle's Nest the men take note of the indicators of the recent presence of their now absent enemies. Everywhere the sense of abandonment is fresh. The open registration book for the luxurious hotel at the foot of the mountain lists the names of Nazi notables. The staff is putting out formal silver place settings in the dining room. Eagle's Nest, spare but majestic, contains Hitler's personal photo album, and we look at its snapshots over the shoulder of the GI who finds it first. The men commandeer Mercedes staff cars and trucks with the Nazi flags affixed. Winters pulls Nixon away from the Eagle's Nest balcony, with its spectacular mountaintop view of the Alps, the valleys, and the water below, to give him the "present" of Goering's wine cellar. In one of the most emphatic point of view set-ups in the episode, Nixon stops to stare, transfixed, at the vast, multi-story warehouse holding thousands of racks of Europe's finest vintages. The tasting tables still have bottles open upon them. Easy Company here witnesses the Third Reich's vision of power in its fusion of natural beauty and material wealth. Eagle's Nest associates the grandeur of the Third Reich's political ambition with the power of nature itself. The outcome of the war, however, has shown the equation of nature and Nazi ideology to be false. The presence of the Nazi regime only in the vestiges of its residence here proves the failure of its vision.

The momentousness of the act of witness becomes even more emphatic through repetition. The next discovery becomes even more spectacular than the one before it. In "Why We Fight" part of the answer to the question the episode title raises comes through the repetition of witnessing, not just by the American soldiers, but more importantly, by the German villagers. Their town at first seems intact, and the fullness of its spaces and inhabitants contrasts completely with the vacant, damaged bodies of the camp survivors. The American military orders the townspeople to go out to the camp, since they deny its existence, and bury the dead. Nixon again walks through the scene, and we see through his eyes the formerly comfortable, middle-class residents of the town forced to confront the consequences of their politics. His gaze falls on women, then an older man who handles corpses while dressed in bowler and topcoat. Nixon encounters a widow whose house he requisitioned the day before. She stared at him unblinkingly in their first confrontation; now she lowers her eyes as she struggles to work in a pile of the dead. The dual witnessing—GIs and German civilians—marks the magnitude of the event, and positions the testimony of witnesses as a source of truth about these events.[162]

Throughout the series interviews with Easy Company veterans frame by preceding (with one exception) the performance of what the men witnessed. Interviews reassert the power of what was witnessed *then* with the authenticity of what survivor-witnesses will testify to *now*. The interviews with the real-life principals warrant the claims of witness testimony as living history. For these last two episodes the veterans' statements reiterate and focus the import of witnessing literally momentous events. The interview comments that begin "Why We Fight" address how the German soldiers the men fought were much like themselves: they were "kids," just "doing a job." They could have been friends, one speculates; they can imagine that they might have enjoyed the same kind of hunting and fishing hobbies as their American counterparts. To begin with commentary that sees the possible common ground between the individual German and American soldiers underlines ironically the discovery of the atrocities that the episode then unfolds. How can human beings do this to each other? What must be the consequences? "Why We Fight" accordingly encompasses other ironies as a result. The chapter begins and ends with a string quartet playing Beethoven while German civilians work on clearing away the rubble of their town. The beauty, timelessness, and classical order of the music contradict the horror and destruction of the scene it accompanies. Before they discover the concentration camp, as Easy Company drives past hundreds of German soldiers who have surrendered, Webster, one of the GIs, shouts at them, "What have you done? What are we doing here?" Landsberg, the village they occupy, appears otherwise normal in every way. Nixon examines desks in an office before entering the well-to-do, well-kept, equally orderly home of the German widow. The middle-class well-being and normality of the village will no longer be able to ignore the horrific abnormality and deprivation of the concentration camp nearby. The overweight baker fights having his supplies and baked goods taken (by Webster) to feed the starving camp inmates. The battalion surgeon, however, to the anguish of the men orders the GIs to stop feeding the requisitioned bread to the starving prisoners because it may kill them. The liberated inmates need to be locked back up in the camp so they can be cared for. The GIs can only help by not helping.

"Points," as the last episode, is the only one that concludes, rather than begins with interviews. The various comments begin and end with statements by Richard Winters, they include the "band of brothers" quotation from Shakespeare's *Henry V*, and in sum the interviewees agree that their service was a privilege because of the group they all served with. Given that the series as a whole focuses on rescue in some form in every episode, the thrust of witness here attests to what was necessary for rescue to occur. The experience of Easy Company testifies to the value of a democracy when it is truly participatory. The combination of performed and actual testimony considers both the possible fallibility and potential strengths of allegiance to a group when it exists to serve ideals, while also insisting those ideals be scrutinized.

The testimony of the real-life principals throughout reasserts the presence of the past, and warrants the process of bearing witness that the series argues is essential to understanding the meaning of World War Two. As the concluding episodes of *Band* suggest, bearing witness becomes a means to reclaim both the time and the space of the past. Bearing witness becomes a means to mark the historic reality of wrongs that occurred during the times and places of the war. The act of witness, as re-created here, becomes the first, necessary step in victory. We see victory as the places of the war purged, redeemed, rescued finally from the evil and wrongdoing that had occupied them. Witnessing in *Band* returns the past, and articulates the meaning of events. Witness becomes a necessary condition of rescue and redemption of space and time. Through witness we understand in moral terms why it was and what it was that these men fought for.

The witnesses in *Band* are also survivors. *Band*, we believe, achieves something genuinely innovative—it re-articulates the figure of the

Survivor, allowing memorialization to become testimony-led. *Saving Private Ryan* also presented a "Now" figure to set against those portrayed living and dying "Then." The scenes in which the older Ryan, infirm, and near his own end, visits with his family the iconic Omaha Beach cemetery in Normandy are typically Spielbergian to some (given their potentially embarrassing sentimentality). But they are there to open a perspective on the events of the war. The older Ryan, aware in this setting of death that he has lived a life that others were never permitted to live, articulates an archetypal Survivor's guilt when he begs his wife, "Tell me that I've been a good man!" The film's project is to attempt to memorialize, and in so doing re-assess, "goodness" of (and in) War.

But the older Ryan (Hamilton Young) and the younger Ryan (Matt Damon) are both *actors*. In *Band*, by contrast, the testimony of the veterans that begins each episode adds a sober, documentary *frame* lacking in the cinema feature. There is no need for the "Tell me I've been a good man" emotional imperative of the feature film—an audience must judge what sort of men these are from their self-presentation (their physical address to the camera and the words they speak). In Part 10, there is a final resonance to this trope, when testimony is re-situated in valedictory conclusion to the dramatic action. When the old soldiers speak at any time in the series the address to the audience shifts and new questions are posed. Living presences perform with absent presences shadowing their image. This kind of witness statement may not be new—Warren Beatty's 1981 *Reds* used footage of old timers' interviews to add distance to the story of Jack Reed and the Russian Revolution—but it is a relatively new feature of TV docudrama, and as Robert Rosenstone has argued in the case of *Reds*, the interviews "provide a context for and a commentary on the dramatic scenes.[163] If the purpose of testimony in *Reds* is to offer "competing voices" that sometimes go against the grain of the drama,[164] *Band* gives its old timers a platform from which their continuing "brotherhood" can speak to—and with—the action.

The use of direct address testimony marks the series as a docudrama intertextual with documentary representations of war. In common with television documentary, the presence of the older men—the Private Ryans grown old—works to frame the television drama in a qualitatively different way from the film. In addition to allowing the resolution of each narrative segment to articulate the significance of the events that have been re-created, each episode of *Band* begins with interviews with the real-life principals whose stories are about to be re-enacted. These interview segments echo the structure of Stephen Ambrose's book (and are a visual figure for his research methodology). They headline the claims the work is making about the need for making war and the impact on these particular combatants of the fact of making war. The metaphorical emphasis on the "brotherhood" the men in Easy Company experience is underscored by *evidence*. This is foregrounded both at source (Ambrose's book) and within the diegesis of the miniseries (the primary documentary interviews framing the dramatic episodes). A perspective is thereby gained on the fact of that comradeship, on the power of its continuation, and on its implications in and for the Here and Now. "Rescue" as a recurring value in the miniseries results in part from the treatment of the group more as a *family* who are attempting to survive in world of graphically re-created violence. On one hand, the consistent envisioning of leadership as a means of rescue links *Band* to other father/son/family configurations that recur so often in Spielberg films. On the other hand, like the reiteration of "brotherhood" and bonding that emerges from the Ambrose text, angles of coherence, lines of intelligibility emerge from which these respective works articulate the meaning of their historical material.

The European Context

Band of Brothers, then, uses the enhanced strategies of modern docudrama in order in part to respond to the concerns of a post-September 11 American culture. Such a prestigious miniseries would be unthinkable in conventional TV budget terms whether in America or elsewhere. Even in America the project might not have acquired financial critical mass were it not for the name Spielberg. Once that name is there, however, it easily becomes "the kind of TV project that comes along once in a generation...With a $120 million dollar budget, DreamWorks could afford to shoot big crowds on accurate locations, and to spend months in the studio at Hatfield."[165]

However, as Ebbrecht has shown,[166] European "Public Service" television docudrama, or "Historical-Event Television," has in recent years also re-situated historical events through representation. The formal hybridization evident in Historical-Event Television, expanding the palette of the television docudrama at the "high concept" end of production, demonstrates a remarkable synergy with *Band of Brothers*. Docudrama, a venerable European TV form, thus finds itself in an interesting position ethically in relation to the current, reality-soaked, TV culture. The maximizing of the act of witness both in performance and reception evident in the New Docudrama is a good fit with what Dovey has identified as the tendency towards "First Person" address in television.[167] This address can have the effect of magnifying the individual over against the collective. It is, as Dovey argues, very much of our time, and in the New Docudrama a kind of triangulation is effected by three highly active current modes:

—first-person witness – the recounting of actual testimony (the documentary base),

—actors bearing witness as dramatic protagonists (*enacting* a script based on testimony),

—audience witness (the context of reception as memorialization/ reflection).

Band of Brothers exhibits and exploits the emotional power inherent in act(s) of witness. British director David Leland, responsible for one of the strongest evocations of Easy Company's war in the "Bastogne" episode, observed, "We're representing the experiences of men *whose faces* appear at the beginning of every episode. They are real people, and we had *a duty* to tell their story faithfully."[168]   The moral imperative expressed here echoes that of the Survivor figure, whose "face" is, or can be, a profound signifier in a world grown suspicious of language.

Writing about Peter Watkins' 1964 *Culloden*, John Corner describes its poetics as "a strategic mix of closeness and distance." On the one hand, he says, the film "pull[s] the viewer into an *emotionally turbulent* act of witness;" on the other it is a "tart lesson" in history.[169] He has recently amplified his thoughts about the potential of docudrama as follows: "Because of its diegetic character, dramadoc can provide modes of sensory engagement with the specificities of 'living' more intimately and continuously than most conventional documentary formats can, albeit with some licence."[170]

Closeness and distance define the twin imperatives of performance in historical event-television. In relation to German television practice since the mid-1990s, Ebbrecht identifies oral history as the major means by which a "personalization and individualization of history" has achieved closeness. "[I]nterviews with so-called *Zeitzeugen*, or eyewitnesses," he observes, is: "the basic principle…These witnesses *become the protagonists* of historical event-television."[171]

Witness testimony has become a central convention of modern historical event docudrama.[172] The act of witness partly facilitates what Ebbrecht calls a "re-dramatization of history." This re-inflects "actual political and social incidents, interpretations and discourses" to become "part of collective memory" within a national culture."[173] He observes that "many more interview sequences [are] now integrated into the narrative,"[174] noting this as "a reflection of the new prominence of oral history from the 1960s."

The act of witness, made central to the re-framing of history, heralds a Return of the Documentary Repressed for the docudrama. But other refinements also make major contributions to New Docudrama's project of re-forming popular history. The films:

—tell stories that meet popular expectations and reflect current debates
—reproduce cinema aesthetics
—focus on popular actors.

Through these means the codes and conventions of docudrama (as outlined by Paget 1998; Lipkin 2002) have been fundamentally extended and re-articulated for a new conjuncture. In the best examples of practice, docudrama has moved decisively backwards—in the direction of the documentary evidence from whence it originated. In the first instance, the films capitalize on "history as current event" in the public sphere "because of anniversaries or rising public interest in specific historic topics."[175] Secondly, "a fluent and popular narration...activates the emotional sense of the audience" and smoothes the way to higher ratings by means of intertextuality with the well known tropes of feature filmmaking.[176] Thirdly, actors (also often well known to their audience from other dramas) facilitate the desired ratings precisely by "becom[ing] part of contemporary memory culture"[177] through suture with witness testimony. Young performers mirror by enactment the tales to which older witnesses have testified in a kind of double "warranting." The current age of the speaker(s), and their relation to the current age of the witness(es), encourages audience identification at several personal, historical and ethical levels. This "Young/Old: Then/Now" synthesis "works as an archive of collective memory and at the same time, takes part in the construction of a national culture of public memory."[178]

Conclusion

The emotional pull of the Real is as strong now as it ever was, and the docudrama has found new ways of articulating this. British military historian (and broadcaster) Richard Holmes's account of the Spielberg/Hanks/HBO series puts this succinctly:

> *Band of Brothers* was compelling and compassionate. The series emphasized the commitment of basically decent folk to one another and to winning the war...We are far too close on 11 September to assess it properly. Yet it seems to have regenerated something that we saw at the heart of *Band of Brothers*, that quality of resolve that America's adversaries believed had vanished from the "decadent" west, and without which wars are not won.[179]

World War Two (relatively unproblematic) is held up as the mirror for more problematic conflicts located in a new age. Due *homage* is paid to the historical past and its representatives. But the perspective of elapsed time allows for new questions to be asked in the present through the dialogue the series sets up between Then and Now/Young and Old. This kind of docudrama seeks to be both/and, rather than either/or, documentary and drama, allowing *Band of Brothers* to propose itself as both archive and performance. In so doing, and in outlasting the former "occasional" nature of docudrama on television through a continued existence on DVD and video, docudrama has entered a new phase.

CHAPTER TWELVE

THE RELATABLE REAL: DOCUDRAMA, ETHICS, AND *SAVING JESSICA LYNCH*

In contributing forcefully to the process of shaping public memory docudramas inevitably raise the kinds of ethical questions brought to light by a film such as *United 93*, or incorporates them directly into the exploration of memory offered by works such as *Band of Brothers*, *Defiance* and *Flags of Our Fathers*. The case of *Saving Jessica Lynch* returns us squarely to the ethics of films that are both about and contribute to the process of shaping public memory.

On Sunday night, November 9, 2003, NBC premiered *Saving Jessica Lynch* (P. Markle). As a movie-of-the-week docudrama *Saving Jessica Lynch* re-creates what had been one of the major and more controversial news events of the then weeks-old war in Iraq. Lynch's unit, the 507th Maintenance Company, consisting of a long convoy of supply trucks and repair vehicles, made a series of wrong turns and attempted to go through, rather than around, the city of Nasiriyah. The group was ambushed, with initially sixteen of its members listed as "missing." Several appeared shortly afterward on television as prisoners of war. Lynch, one of the seriously wounded survivors, was taken to an Iraqi hospital. When American forces extracted Lynch from the hospital initial news coverage embraced United States officials' eagerness to headline the heroism of Lynch's resistance to capture, and the apparently daring raid that retrieved her. Jessica Lynch became a news commodity, not only as Operation Iraqi Freedom's first rescued POW, but also as a celebrity. Within weeks she sold her life rights for the production of a movie-of-the-week based on her exploits. *Hustler* publisher Larry Flynt announced he had acquired nude pictures of Lynch. Finally, in the fall of 2003 Lynch's book (*I Am A Soldier, Too: The Jessica Lynch Story*[180]) and NBC's docudrama were offered to the public simultaneously. Numerous web sites appeared examining every facet of Lynch's life, including her wounds, her recuperation, and her wedding plans.[181]

Jessica Lynch remains, perhaps in every sense of the word, one of the more constructed emblems of the Bush administration's post-September 11 conflict of culture: "Jessica Lynch" connotes American innocence used by the forces at war in this conflict, somehow emerging through strength of spirit to resume a normal life as a normal, small-town American. The movie-of-the-week docudrama version of the errors that put Lynch's convoy in the line of fire, and Lynch's subsequent capture and rescue aired a mere seven months after the events it depicts. The film's broadcast, coinciding with the release and promotion of Lynch's story in print, precipitated revisiting charges raised in the media that the United States government had exploited as a propaganda opportunity what had happened to Lynch, as well as any heroism in her service to her country.

The Ethics of Shaping Public Memory

Saving Jessica Lynch draws on two sources for its re-creation of its story, Lynch's memories, and the account offered by Iraqi lawyer Mohammed al-Rehaief of his efforts to provide the American military the information it needed to extract Lynch from the Iraqi hospital where she was being held. True to its form as a movie-of-the-week docudrama, the film narrates the material it documents (it is, as opening credits reminds us, "based on a true story") through the codes and conventions of the classic Hollywood narrative film, drawing on the strategies characteristic of melodrama, and in particular those of stories about victims and the trials they face. The sense of victimization in the film is, however, a two-edged sword. In a key moment, as Lynch's convoy has been decimated, victorious fedayeen shoot the dead, dying, and wounded American soldiers. We see Lynch's body, pulled from the wreckage of a Humvee, sprawled helpless and broken on the street. The fedayeen leader notices that she is conscious, moves closer to her, leans down to her, and says, "Welcome to my country." The scene shows the fedayeen as guerilla fighters, ruthlessly using their streets against an inadequately prepared, out-of-place American force incapable of effectively defending itself. The scene raises the question: what has victimized Lynch and the others? There is a further blending in *Saving Jessica Lynch* of biopic and war story: we see Lynch as small-town girl (flashbacks show us her pre-war life in West Virginia); Lynch as innocent victim/soldier; two different rescue stories (al-Rehaief's story, showing how he assumes great risk to tell the American army where Lynch is, and the story of the army's rescue based on his information); and the larger war story itself. Certainly "embedded" news coverage of the war in Iraq has provided an iconography both of what we believe that country at war looks like, as well as of its American combatants, and the film, shot on location in Texas, adheres faithfully to that "look."

What is at stake, ethically, in the broadcast market's efforts to thrust Jessica Lynch into the culture of war? British theatre historian Derek Paget states in his fifth "Modest Proposal" about docudrama, that "To theatricalize public occurrence is to engage in a mode of aesthetic and ethical inquiry."[182] Paget's proposition identifies what is tantamount to an ethical imperative. In the case of the works presented as movie-of-the-week docudramas on American television, an ethical imperative suggests that these are stories that should be told, and told this way. The proposition invites us to confront the purposes and effects of docudrama. Why might one particular story be exemplary? What results when a story is offered to the world as itself "based on a true story"? What docudramas are and what they do create at least three fundamental areas of ethical consideration that I will examine below. It is first necessary to view American MOW docudramas as "documents." Representing actual people, places, and events traditionally has been the work of documentary film. Docudramas, in part, share this work as a function of their storytelling. Here their proximity to actuality shapes the site of the ethical debate that arises. Second, docudramas are also persuasive appeals. The warranting strategies they incorporate invite examining their means of ethical persuasion. "Warrants" through a basis in common sense and logic, provide the means to allow arguments to reason from evidence to the conclusions they advocate. Finally, American movie-of-the-week docudramas function as products, produced because they are "rootable" (tied to known events), "relatable" (appealing to the core of the TV audience), and "promotable" (easy for networks to sell).[183] Ethical concerns grow out of the appropriateness of commodifying life stories, as well as the process of legitimizing legal, political, social, and moral issues that become viewed through the prism of commodification. In what ways does selling *Saving Jessica Lynch* as a movie-of-the-week docudrama serve the interests of its network, of viewers, of voters, of the Pentagon, the policies of the Bush administration, not to mention Jessica Lynch herself? NBC's November, 2003 broadcast of *Saving Jessica Lynch* will, as a MOW and as an event (broadcast the Sunday night before Veterans Day; broadcast at the outset of a week of talk show appearances by Lynch to plug her book) serve as a case study to illuminate these perspectives and to suggest that the work allows for varied readings of what it advocates.

1. *Saving Jessica Lynch* as Document

Docudramas argue initially that we need to receive them as a mixture of presentational modes. Docudramas indicate their roots in actuality when they are "based on" or "inspired by" "true stories." The "narrative of a narrative" the assertion presents us with, that the story we're about to see is itself "based on a true story," signals clearly that the work before us is an adaptation, often of a well-known prior text or a publicly-known event that has been widely reported. The story *Saving Jessica Lynch* tells us began when the news media heavily publicized Lynch's capture and subsequent extraction from an Iraqi hospital in late March and early April, 2003.

Initial news stories about the attack on Lynch's convoy, her capture, and her rescue emphasized armed resistance. For example, BBC news noted that:

> "There is as yet no clear picture of the circumstances of her capture, but intelligence suggests Private Lynch fought a heroic battle," U.S. officials told the *Washington Post* newspaper. "Ambushed by Iraqi forces, she continued firing back even after she had already been hit multiple times herself and had seen several other soldiers in her unit die around her," one official told the paper. "She was fighting to the death," the official said. "She did not want to be taken alive."[184]

The same theme of armed resistance appeared in the first reports of Lynch's rescue: "The troops fought their way into the hospital and whisked Lynch away on a stretcher, fighting their way out."[185]

By mid-May, the BBC challenged the claims of the original coverage as "one of the most stunning pieces of news management yet conceived."[186] For a time, the BBC pushed hard the argument that the Pentagon had "wagged the dog" in its readiness to "produce" the Jessica Lynch story as an episode in a war narrative it could shape. The BBC placed the packaging of the video of the rescue from the hospital in the context of an earlier collaboration of the Pentagon with producer/director Jerry Bruckheimer. This was a reality TV show based on a series of stories about soldiers in Afghanistan, "Profiles From the Front Line."[187] Bruckheimer two years previously had produced *Black Hawk Down*. NBC's eventual adaptation limits its narrative scope to re-creating what happened to Lynch, rather than widening its view to encompass any analysis or assessment of the accompanying news coverage, the claims about the "staged" elements of the rescue, and the controversies these generated, as a documentary might about the same subject.

Even more, in this case we clearly are only partly in the realm of truth claims made by documentary, because movie-of-the-week docudramas indicate to their audiences the need to receive them as entertainment products. Docudramas enter the market place as feature films and movie-of-the-week presentations and narrate their actual material through the codes and conventions of drama and melodrama. What results is a fusion of documentary and narrative modes of presentation, and in this case in particular, a blending of the journalistic (news stories), the personal (Lynch's and al-Rehaief's stories), and Hollywood, movie-of-the-week stylization.

Through their basis in true stories docudramas claim that what we are about to see on screen happened much like what transpired in actuality. The prior text(s) that provides the basis for the docudrama story will motivate the narrative's resemblances to its referents. Consequently narrative representation re-creates as closely as possible what we know about the actuality it re-presents. In semiotic terms, docudrama's hybridity depends upon indexical icons, re-creations that bear close, motivated resemblances to the real.[188] Docudrama's rhetorical integrity, its validity as argument, depends entirely then on the extent to which it can substantiate the proximity it claims to its subject matter.

2: *Saving Jessica Lynch* as Persuasive Argument

Proximity strategies in docudrama provide rhetorical warrants, allowing the films to make claims about their subjects based on the data, the documentary subject matter, they re-create.[189] Docudramatic rhetoric uses several kinds of warrants to connect its presentation of its subjects to the claims the narratives forward.[190] Most predominantly, works construct models of the people, places, and events that make up their stories. Models bear directly motivated resemblances to their subject. Modeling warrants are as evident in the casting of principal parts as they are in the re-creation of key locations and the iconography of events. In this instance NBC re-created the images of Jessica Lynch that would be highly familiar to the audience for the work, including the service portrait that had appeared on news magazine covers, and the wire-service frame grab of Lynch on a cot being removed from the Iraqi hospital.

The proximity strategies docudramas employ both influence and warrant the arguments the films would forward about their subjects. With some docudramas, critics raise ethical red flags when the degree of proximity becomes questionable.[191] In this case CBS dropped initial plans for a Lynch docudrama because of the controversy surrounding the facts of both capture and rescue. NBC's eventual production avoided the errors of early April's news coverage, avoided the speculative re-creation of the disputed, abusive treatment Lynch may or may not have received between capture and hospital internment, and split its viewpoint between Lynch's conscious memory, and the account of her rescue marketed by Mohammed al-Rehaief, the Iraqi lawyer who directed the American army to Lynch's hospital room.

3: *Saving Jessica Lynch* as Product

Movie-of-the-week docudrama has been a staple of telefilm production since the 1980s. ABC, CBS and NBC invested in docudrama production through the 1990s in an effort to counter the loss of their audience to cable. What television executives, producers and writers have termed the "rootable," "relatable," and "promotable" qualities of docudrama properties have made the production of movies based on true stories a key strategy during sweeps periods for attracting and retaining audience. Due to its "rootable" material—the widely known, the frequently current, and the often notorious nature of its subject matter—docudrama can be convenient to promote. The desire for "relatable" material has led to narrower choices of subject matter. In marketing terms "relatability" tends to put white, middle-class, female central characters in some form of jeopardy. The preference for stories "based on" or "inspired by" actual events—often with female central characters—reflects directly the ongoing effort by both network and cable to win, recapture and maintain what they define as the core of their target audience, women between the ages of 18 and 49. In these terms, *Saving Jessica Lynch* represents an ideal MOW docudrama property.

To put *Saving Jessica Lynch* in context, a sampling of concurrent sweeps period programming illustrates the range of central characters, actual circumstances and arguments advocated in MOW docudramatic practice. During the May 2003 sweeps, just weeks after the invasion of Iraq began, American networks programmed no less than seven MOW docudramas, including a two-night miniseries, *Hitler: The Rise of Evil*. Of the seven titles, three centered on war or war-related stories (*Hitler*; *Out of the Ashes*; and *Daughter from Da Nang*). Three others gave the "inside" stories of famous subjects (*Lucy*; *Behind the Camera: 3's Company, The Unauthorized Story*; *Martha Inc.*) Two of the MOW docudramas coat-tailed prominent news events (*Martha Inc.*; *Ice Bound*). This typology is typical of network MOW production through the early

2000s. The sampling's emphasis on war subjects is characteristic of sweeps docudrama programming between 2000 and 2004.[192]

It should not be surprising that as rootable, relatable, and promotable products, American MOW docudramas after 9/11 should turn to war-related topics and visions of rescuing Americans and American interests.[193] Similar in this respect to *Band of Brothers*, *Saving Jessica Lynch* argues not only that in the post-9/11 world we necessarily see rescuers (and the rescued) as heroes, but also begs for the nobility of a war that is necessary to rescue Americans, American interests, and ultimately, some sense of our identity as Americans.

This, however, is one view. Consider another. Jessica Lynch is "rescued" not simply from a desperate, life-threatening combat situation, but also from an erroneous national policy. Early in the film we see Lynch's convoy approaching, and then entering the city of Nasiriyah. Scenes just before this have re-created the fateful, erroneous decisions to make the wrong turns that have brought the convoy to this juncture. As the heavy trucks and Humvees slowly make their way through the streets the surprised townspeople watch its progress. The American soldiers nervously study the Iraqis in return. The mutual apprehension and the point of view structure build systematically, culminating in an exchange of glances between Lynch and an Iraqi man in a pick-up truck that begins to shadow the convoy. In slow motion, the man opens a cell phone and begins to speak. The convoy unsuccessfully attempts to turn around and retreat, but a school bus is pushed across the street, blocking their escape.

The film shows American troops being attacked. Re-creating the attack on Jessica Lynch's convoy also necessitates showing American troops in a place they do not belong. They are, quite simply, invaders who are being attacked. Is the action then self-defense, or is it aggression? *Saving Jessica Lynch* invites—and warrants—divergent readings, interpretations of what it shows that both support and criticize the presence of the American army in Iraq. In both views, as it offers persuasive argument the film re-creates events to provide necessary data, and uses its re-creation of physical damage to actual individuals to warrant larger arguments about national policy and national identity. Pentagon control over images of the war underlines the necessity of re-creating events. As much as "Operation Iraqi Freedom" has been given air time in the media, that effort to control how the war appears has been evident from the outset in "embedded" news reporting, and through the kinds of images the Pentagon itself generates ("Mission Accomplished") or restricts. The salience of that control is perhaps most evident when it is breached—when Al-Jazeera becomes the outlet for airing footage no one else has shown, when photos of flag-draped coffins do appear in the media, and when photos of prisoners at Abu Ghraib reach the light of day. As Americans we are, *Saving Jessica Lynch* would argue, both our mistakes and our efforts to correct them. Other recent war docudramas such as *Black Hawk Down* and *We Were Soldiers* raise the same questions, and similarly define national identity through their narratives of necessary rescue. At bottom, these are all stories of the need to rescue who and what we are as a country, a need precipitated by the decision—and the pressure—to go war.

Should this story be told, and told this way? The selling of Jessica Lynch contributed yet another means of keeping George Bush's war in Iraq at the forefront of public debate. While marketed to sell heroism, this docudramatic re-creation also invites the argument that both Americans and Iraqis are victims of the questionable competence of leadership.[194] As a cultural document, *Saving Jessica Lynch* ignores the April news ballyhoo the U.S. government welcomed originally with its erroneous reports lauding heroism under fire. Lynch's subsequent immersion in celebrity in November, 2003—her efforts in interviews and television talk shows to correct the record on her own actions not withstanding[195]—perpetuates a sense of American victimization and rationalized retaliation that propelled Bush administration foreign and domestic policies after 9/11. Lynch herself remains a convenient emblem of violated innocence.

CHAPTER THIRTEEN

THE FAMOUS, THE EXEMPLARY, THE TALENTED, THE COMPULSIVE: TRENDS IN RECENT BIOPICS

"To me a valid fictional character is, in a lot of ways, easier than trying to portray a real character, because you've got the standards of plausibility and recognizing—the amount that people would recognize false notes—in the person you are portraying. Had an actor run away and started doing something with either Jobs or Gates particularly, that just was not consistent with what: A. they are and were, or B. what was known about them by the audience that would be watching this film, that you could lose that audience. Whereas in a fictional character there's no such standards in the back of the audience's mind."
—Martyn Burke, Writer/Director, *Pirates of Silicon Valley*[196]

"For me drama is really about how a character changes, and the only thing that's really compelling in a story is how a character grows. I said, OK, here's an opportunity—if we start Jones as a young boy, see how he became interested in golf, watch him grow from child to adult. Let's see him make that transition into the adult world, take on adult responsibilities. Then let's see him go from adult to leader, leader to champion. Let's see him go from champion to visionary."
—Rowdy Herrington, Writer/Director, *Bobby Jones: Stroke of Genius*[197]

The popularity of the biopic through the 1990s, especially the surge in the cycle between 2000 and 2005, raises several basic questions: why have biographical films been so popular in the post-millennium culture of fame and reality television? What, if anything, do these recent feature film and movie-of-the-week biopics have in common with the classic Hollywood studio biopic of the 30s, 40s, and 50s? Recent works have told the life stories of musicians (*The Pianist*; *Ray*; *De-Lovely*; *Beyond the Sea*; *Walk the Line*), scientists (*A Beautiful Mind*; *Kinsey*), noteworthy figures including conquerors, criminals, and politicians (*Alexander*; *Catch Me If You Can*; *Monster*; *Motorcycle Diaries*; *Good Night, and Good Luck*; *Frost/Nixon*; *Milk*), artists and writers (*Pollock*; *Frida*; *American Splendor*; *Antwone Fisher*; *Finding Neverland*; *Capote*); actors (*Autofocus*; *Confessions of a Dangerous Mind; The Life and Death of Peter Sellers*), and athletes (*Seabiscuit*; *Coach Carter*; *Cinderella Man*; *The Greatest Game Ever Played*)—within this diverse range of life stories, what are the common threads? What structural consistencies within these narratives make the cycle identifiable?

Contemporary biopics exist to explain the fame, the notoriety, and (or) the noteworthiness of their main subject. Given this fundamental purpose their representations strive to make accessible the exceptional. They must re-create as vividly as possible a sense of their subjects' extraordinary abilities and/or accomplishments. What is extraordinary about the subject in many cases is what is most known about them, most public. Accomplishment anchors the film that re-creates the exceptional to actuality itself. While each varied story must offer a different explanation as to why its subject performs in exemplary or extraordinary ways, we come to understand exceptional ability as the product of pressures that are both external (economic, social, and/or political) and internal. Often we see, literally, the inner demons driving the need to perform. The presence of family with its own attendant pressures tends to mediate these external and internal pressures on the performances we witness. In many cases we come to view the ability to excel as a compulsive response to the array of pressures the subject of the story faces. Three very different films about Richard Nixon, for example (*Nixon*; *Frost/Nixon*; *Secret Honor* [R. Altman, 1984]) share a similar view of the disgraced president as both trapped (by physical as well as political circumstances) and driven. Biopics about artists argue from comparable sets of tensions. At bottom, in their views of their subjects' lives, recent biopics explain extraordinary, if not heroic performance as an exemplary response to constraining, even repressive contexts.

Extraordinary Exemplars

The biopic purports to answer the question, why is it worth making and watching a film about this individual? The fundamental claim of the biopic is that what this person did defined who they were or are, and that the film's audience needs to know why the life they will learn about is exemplary. As biopics, these films address the need to explain extraordinary performance. As docudramas, biopics focus the energy of their re-creation on depicting the dynamic interrelationship between pressures and performance. Performance in these cases provides the necessary anchor to actuality that characterizes the arguments they will make as docudramas. Accordingly, extraordinary performance makes for a deserving subject, the films would argue, and at the same time anchors the film in the actuality of our lives. Some of these films build on some degree of fame, while others bring subjects to us that likely we might not know about otherwise. The premise for some of the films, then, is the need to explain a subject who is well known (*Ray*; *The Aviator*), while for others the premise is that the subject of the film is someone who should be known about and now will be (*The Insider*; *The Pianist*; *A Beautiful Mind*; *Catch Me If You Can*; *Cinderella Man; The Greatest Game Ever Played*). In either case the rootability of the film, its anchoring in actuality, is the fact of the extraordinary. The existence of what the subject has accomplished serves to launch the explanation the film gives. Furthermore, the extraordinary roots of the story warrant the subsequent re-creation necessary to the film's style of storytelling. *Ray* (T. Hackford, 2004) and *Walk the Line* (J. Mangold, 2005), for example, purport to provide an opportunity to relive the quality of their subjects' performance through re-creation. The rendering of performance in both depends upon the motivated resemblance of the film actors to the real-life performers' sound and appearance. Their re-creations offer varying degrees of proximity to the originals in both look and sound: while Joaquin Phoenix and Reese Witherspoon are on *Walk The Line*'s soundtrack performing the music of Cash and Carter, Ray Charles re-created his own music for Jamie Foxx to lipsync in *Ray*, placing the claims to represent the real of both films in the echoes of close but clearly marked analogies.

The explanation and consequent understanding that docudramas generally, and biopics in particular promise to deliver necessitates telling the "inside" story of their subject. The films I consider here share the same basic purpose of the classic studio biopic produced by Hollywood between 1920 and 1960, to explain what purports to be a "true version" of the life of an historical person.[198] Reviewers of contemporary biopics foreground as conventions an equation of the stages of an individual's life with narrative arc, so that childhood events (often traumatic), family and marriage (often in turmoil), career setbacks, and the search for redemption carve out the iconography and the recurring ideas characteristic of the genre.[199] Even though they are products of a different production system, contemporary biopics also center on similar components of the construction of fame as did the classic biopic, as we see talented individuals struggling with the exigencies of romantic interests, family pressures, and forums in which they are subject to community judgment.[200] While the classical studio biopic tended to attempt to "'normalize' genius" in depicting "well-adjusted, successful biopic" subjects,[201] however, the contemporary biopic foregrounds the compulsions that drive their characters in the face of personal and social pressures and constraints. If a compulsion is an irresistible impulse to act, then recent biopics argue that we must understand extraordinary performance as the result of pressures that make action necessary, combined with a subject's unique abilities and talents. The results, the films argue, are noteworthy enough that they deserve to become the subjects of a film.

Personal Pressures

Just as the classical biopic depicted, or if necessary, constructed romantic interests for its main character as an element of understanding what life was like for someone who has become famous, recent biopics also incorporate if not center on problematic love lives. This is especially true in *Ray* and *Walk The Line*, as the narrative arcs in the films link the very process of creating the music that made these two performers famous to the women they "performed" with as musicians and lovers, members of the Raylettes in the first case, and June Carter, in the second. *The Aviator* (M. Scorcese, 2004) suggests that Howard Hughes's life was in large part a search for, and the unsuccessful coping with the loss of women who would both love and mother him, beginning with his biological mother, and developing through the periods of his life when he was involved with Katherine Hepburn and Ava Gardner. Both are shown emphatically as mother figures who help restore him physically: the film begins with Hughes's mother bathing him; later we see Hepburn cleaning his wounds after a plane crash; after that, Gardner cleans him up before he must testify before a Congressional committee. From his desires for familial and romantic love and success on the links, desires the film shows *as* linked, Francis Ouimet in *The Greatest Game Ever Played* attempts to court a young woman of the aristocracy, only to find that his presence in her social space—her home, and the country club dance floor—exacerbates her father's and brother's protective opposition to his efforts to cross class barriers. By contrast, in *Bobby Jones: Stroke of* Genius (R. Herrington, 2004) it is golf that threatens the normalcy and stability of the courtship and marriage of Mary and Bobby Jones. The fact that the couple makes their marriage their top priority ironically becomes what allows Jones to act on his compulsive need to play, to win the Grand Slam, and, in essence, to get over it.

For contemporary biopics showing "what really happened" tends to center on the psychology, the inner pressures, sometimes literally the inner demons that drive the subjects of their stories and motivate their desire to achieve. Internal pressures often become evident as compulsions driving the subjects of the films. *Nixon* and *Frost/Nixon* both suggest Richard Nixon is driven by guilt: over the loss of the presidency, the loss (again) in politics to his inferiors, and (as we see with others) the deaths of his brothers. In some cases the inner pressure driving characters is relatable fear, such as the fear for one's family in *Cinderella Man*, or the fear for one's life and loved ones that we see in *The Pianist*. In *A Beautiful Mind* (R. Howard, 2001) John Nash's search for patterns becomes shockingly graphic in the crazy quilt collage of newspaper and magazine articles he plasters over the walls of his garage. The films depict creativity as compulsive behavior. Artists Jackson Pollock and Frida Kalo are driven to create despite (or because of) the constraints of emotional circumstances, and in Kalo's case, physical pain and debilitation. The spontaneous improvisational creation of music in *Ray* and performances in *Walk the Line* offer the lighter side of a compulsion the film argues is driven by survivor guilt, drugs, and irrepressible sexual desire. Similarly we see J.M. Barrie's impulsive creation of improvisational scenes in *Finding Neverland* (M. Forster, 2004) serves as therapeutic amusement for the boys he wants to befriend. In these cases the people we're learning about simply can't help what they do, and when they do it, the results are extraordinary.

Bobby Jones suggests its main character (James Caviezel) is driven from childhood through golf to overcome his own temper (swearing, throwing clubs), his own physical limitations (a neurological disorder), and challenges to judgment posed by courses (recurring bunker shots) and opponents (Walter Hagen's psychological hazing of a lesser-experienced Jones). *The Greatest Game* shows the inner demons that drive the competitors literally as ghosts that haunt the course and threaten their necessary abilities to concentrate, to focus, and to visualize. In *Cinderella Man* (R. Howard, 2005), the subjective inserts of Braddock's (Russell

Crowe) children never disrupt but instead sharpen his ability to refocus on his opponent. Here the compulsive appearances of the spirits that visit the performers are literally distractions to the crucial processes of visualization and consequently compel even higher levels of concentration. Vardon, we learn, was evicted from his family home as a young child because the land they farmed was condemned, seized, and built into a golf course. His inner demons appear as cut-aways to his memories of the black stove-pipe hatted surveyors who were the first indication that his life was to change course. Oiumet (Shia LaBeouf) grows up in similar circumstances, his family home sits just across the road from the Brookline Country Club where he works as a caddy and strives to be part of the U.S. Open, the "greatest game ever played." The image that indicates the internal pressures Ouimet must manage becomes the sight of his father in the gallery. His father believes golf is a worthless distraction from what the boy really needs to do, which is to help support his economically marginal family, and has issued an ultimatum that failing to win will mean giving up the game for good to fulfill the greater obligation. Ouimet, however, is "called" to the game at a very early age—we see him breaking "house rules" night after night, practicing putting on his hardwood bedroom floor, perfecting the stroke of a peculiarly breaking putt that we will later see him have to make at a crucial, late stage in his quest to win the Open. The film suggests that his ability to perform is the fruit of both pressures, his compulsion to perfect his skill at the game, and the need forced upon him to prove that skill to a disapproving father.

While the traditional classic studio biopic tended to minimize and standardize the roles families played for their main characters,[202] in many contemporary biopics we come to understand performance as a result of characters internalizing family stresses. John Nash's compulsive search for patterns competes with a normal, family life, and threatens to distance him so fully from reality that eventually he fears he will harm his infant son. The main character in *Catch Me If You Can* (S. Spielberg, 2002) reacts to his salesman father's inadequacy, the resulting loss of family stability, and his mother's infidelity to the father he loves so profoundly by escaping into skillfully created, fraudulent new identities. James Braddock in *Cinderella Man* boxes to earn money to keep his family together, a promise he has made to his children to allay their fears, so that their fears become his. The fear of losing his family frames his fear of being killed in the ring. The films in this group about musicians suggest that their music becomes a means of coping with the loss of family. Szpilman (Adrien Brody) in *The Pianist* suffers from survivor guilt after a friend pulls him from the line of deportees and he watches, helplessly, while the Nazis ship his family off to a concentration camp. *Ray* and *Walk the Line* argue that both musicians suffer persistently from the guilt of inadvertently allowing their brothers to die in accidents they might have somehow prevented. As an appropriate follow-up for DiCaprio's work in *Catch Me*, *The Aviator* similarly explains Howard Hughes's life as a driven search for family and flawlessness through work and lovers. It begins with Hughes as a young boy being bathed by his mother as they spell out "q-u-a-r-a-n-t-i-n-e." Hughes's compulsiveness becomes reiterated in other bathroom scenes in the film, when, for example, he brings his own bar of black soap to the Cocoanut Grove, washes his hands until they bleed, and is temporarily stymied by another bathroom patron touching the doorknob before the now-sterile Hughes hand can turn it to exit. One scene in the film cuts from Hughes stroking the body of his lover to the body of the aircraft he is building. His father is present in the film only in the form of the fortune he leaves his son, who uses it to pursue perfection in the bodies of his films, his women, his aircraft, and in alleviating (or succumbing to) his fear of germs and contamination.

External Pressures

The explanations the films offer of why their subjects perform in extraordinary ways tend to balance inner stresses and external constraints, showing the pressures that motivate these characters to be a response to economic, social, and political exigencies. The ability to perform we see in musicians and athletes tends to be born of the need to escape a life of subsistence: Braddock's career slide in *Cinderella Man* coincides with the onslaught of the Great Depression, so that he foregoes his own food, giving it to his daughter, and fights to keep his children while trying to put meals on the table. Ray Charles takes a bus away from the poverty of the south to perform in the cities of the north; also in the south, Johnny Cash, like James Braddock, is struggling to provide for a wife and young children and somehow establish himself as a performer. *The Greatest Game* similarly shows poverty impelling performance.

For many of the subjects of these films, a marginal economic existence is exacerbated by social discrimination. Braddock must literally bend his head in shame and pass his hat around the fat cats lounging at the boxing commission club to raise enough cash to get the gas in their flat turned back on to bring his children home. Despite how sublime their skills are, Henry Vardon and Francis Ouimet both experience the distaste of the upper class when it is forced to share the golf course and clubhouse with the likes of a "professional" golfer and a caddy. Even Howard Hughes, as an inexperienced Hollywood outsider, runs up against the dismissiveness of Louis B. Mayer and the rest of MGM's upper management when he tries to borrow some cameras. Several others of these films also show performance arising from the need to overcome broader, social and political repression: Edward R. Murrow takes a lone, heroic stance against Joseph McCarthy and his investigatory steamroller; Jeffrey Wigand in *The Insider* holds his own against big tobacco money and the questionable support CBS allows him in trying to go public; Nash in *A Beautiful Mind* believes his efforts in decoding embedded media messages contribute to his country's efforts in the Cold War; the Pianist struggles to survive the nightmare of years of hiding from the Nazis during the Holocaust; Professor Kinsey's compulsively exhaustive survey of sexual practices shatters the pretenses of a repressive fifties American political morality, underlining the film's relevance for the conservative strains of the Bush-era culture. Oliver Stone's *Nixon* (1995) argues, rightly or wrongly, that Nixon was himself a victim, rather than one of the fundamental perpetrators, of the war in Vietnam, indicating the importance of this convention in the contemporary biopic.

The example of *Nixon* shows how literal and figurative trials subject the characters of these films to the pressures of community judgment, not only as performers who wish to succeed with an audience, but human beings whose sense of worth hangs in the balance. Both Ray Charles and Johnny Cash are arrested for drug possession, wreaking havoc with their family lives and suffering blows as a result to their prestige; Hughes's appearances before the Breen Committee as a Hollywood producer to defend the visibility of breasts in his films, and later before a congressional committee investigating his deliveries on contracts during the war, test and evaluate his integrity as a public figure. Athletes such as James Braddock, Bobby Jones, and Francis Ouimet place their ability to perform directly before their audiences, who embody the pressure and presence of community judgment on the quality of what they are offered.

It may be inherent to the form of the biopic in its need to justify its focus on the exemplary individual to argue that noteworthy performance arises as a response to repressive, constraining circumstances and contexts. One final example will suffice to suggest how pervasive as a structuring tension in the biopic may be the interplay between performance and that which would restrain it. There is a moment in *Ray* when a club owner insists on getting the last few minutes of the contracted time or he won't pay the group. In response Charles launches on the spur of the moment into a brand new, previously unheard tune that eventually will become one of his many well-known hits ("What'd I Say?"). The scene argues that here Charles's creativity is spontaneous. The music apparently springs from nowhere indicated or motivated previously, other than Charles and his well of creative resources. Economic pressure, the threat of nonpayment, impels this particular performance, however it is one example of what the film suggests was an ongoing dynamic: Charles's artistry existed both because of and often in spite of the power relations in the world of music that determined his opportunities to perform. We see it in passing in this scene, but also earlier in the exploitative first manager he eventually breaks free from; the sexual liaisons with his co-performers that inspire and distract, energize and drain; the Georgia concert boycott; and the unprecedented ownership Charles eventually negotiated with his recording company over the masters of his albums. Consequently the extraordinary improvisation of "What'd I Say?" arises out of both nothing and everything that has put Charles in front of that audience at that moment. It is but one example of what contemporary biopics argue generally, that extraordinary performance arises, because it must, as a response to all that would hold it back.

CHAPTER FOURTEEN

BRAVE, BATTERED, BUT NOT BARTERED: *GOOD NIGHT, AND GOOD LUCK*, AND THE ARENA OF THE BIOPIC

Even though they are products of a different production system, contemporary biopics also center on similar components of the construction of fame as did the classic biopic, as we see talented individuals struggling with the exigencies of romantic interests, family pressures, and forums in which they are subject to community judgment.[203] The previous chapter examined how, in contrast to the traditional biopic's efforts to show the normalcy of its subjects,[204] the contemporary biopic foregrounds the compulsions that drive their characters in the face of personal and social pressures and constraints. If a compulsion is an irresistible impulse to act, then recent biopics argue that we must understand extraordinary performance as the result of pressures that make action necessary, combined with a subject's unique abilities and talents. The results, the films argue, are noteworthy enough that they deserve to become the subjects of a film.

George Clooney's *Good Night, and Good Luck* (2005), serves to exemplify how contemporary biopics portray exceptional ability as the product of internal and external constraints. In performing Edward R. Murrow's performance as CBS's pre-eminent broadcast journalist of the early 1950s, the film recovers and examines the sources of public memory, much in the way that *Flags Of Our Fathers* details the process that transformed a news photograph into a cultural icon. The film's performance of Murrow and his work also exemplifies the larger notion here of docudrama as the performance of memory. Re-creating Murrow and his work results from the reciprocal legibility of David Strathairn's embodiment of Murrow's gaze, posture, and vocal manner, but only as this enactment resonates within the claustrophobic visual atmosphere of 1950s television, a business itself closely interrelated with the repressive political atmosphere of the United States in the 1950s.

Biopics traditionally offer an explanation of the overall arc of the life of their subject. *Good Night, and Good Luck* more prudently chooses to focus on a defining episode in the life of Edward R. Murrow, perhaps the best-known broadcast journalist of his time. The film focuses on the series of *See It Now* broadcasts in which Murrow, in a way no one before him had possessed the courage or the capacity to do, took the most publicly possible kind of stance against the investigative tactics of Senator Joseph McCarthy. *Good Night* undertakes to explain the nature of Murrow's actions in three ways: first, the film characterizes the series of programs that Murrow is perhaps most famous for as a form of courage under fire. This narrative choice is appropriate, of course, since Murrow became known throughout the world because of his broadcasts from the roof of the BBC during the Blitz. Second, the film examines and illustrates what motivates this courage, showing how Murrow's performance is a response to fear. Third, the film renders cinematically the external threats that created the fearsome atmosphere of institutional repression the *See It Now* broadcasts addressed. The thrust of the film's explanation of Murrow's accomplishment—the quality of his performance at this moment—is to show how the need to take a stand resulted from both internal and external pressures.

Post-war Courage Under Fire

Good Night's explanation balances the larger issues motivating the McCarthy broadcasts against the personal stakes at risk for Murrow when *See It Now* broadcast the programs. The film shows how the features run between late 1953 and 1954 covering the court martial of Milo Radulovich (*The Case Against Milo Radulovich A0589839*), the testimony of Annie Lee Moss before McCarthy's House committee, and the programs specifically devoted to McCarthy (*Report on Senator McCarthy* and McCarthy's response) grew out of a series of efforts to point out the abuse of institutional power in investigations of alleged Communist influence, and the loss of constitutional rights resulting from that abuse. This succession also shows how personal the need to take a stand on principle became for Murrow.

Most agree that Murrow's *See It Now* broadcasts on McCarthy are the most well-known, and probably the most significant of his contributions in television news.[205] *Good Night* has placed at the climax of the development of its story the most historically visible moment in Murrow's work. The film shows the McCarthy programs as the culmination in a succession of hearings, progressing through the due process issues raised by the Air Force's treatment of Radulovich, and the House sub-committee's interrogation of Moss.[206] Re-creating the Radulovich and Moss programs sets up the sense of the individual caught up and victimized by the unfair exercise of institutional power by both framing and giving ample screen space to the archive material from the original programs. In the case of the Moss broadcast, for example, we see some of her testimony, with much of the key moment intact when Senator John McClellan rises to defend Moss against the damaging, unsubstantiated, and unretractable claims made against her by McCarthy's mouthpiece, Roy Cohn. While McClellan speaks with some dismay of the irreparable harm being done to Moss by this treatment, the camera at the hearing pans several times to McCarthy's empty chair, suggesting his cowardly denial of Moss's right to face her accuser in a proper legal forum. *Good Night* similarly emphasizes the original program material from the Radulovich broadcast, following up a long clip of Radulovich's simple but eloquent analysis of the injustice being done to him by holding him responsible for what his father might have read ("Where will all this stop? With my children? With their children?") with shorter interview statements with his father and sister. The clip recurs several times in *Good Night*, reiterating how the program allows Radulovich the opportunity to speak for himself that his court martial has denied him. To achieve the balance of the personal and the historical, the film then frames Radulovich's testimony with its re-creation of Murrow's commentary, which articulates emphatically how the denial of due process has victimized not only Radulovich, but potentially anyone who becomes subject to this form of paranoid persecution. The re-creation highlights what television could do so effectively at this moment, in presenting through a screen suited to the scale of the human face the stories of everyday individuals, easily relatable to the television audience, who as specific victims could throw into sharp relief the moral, legal, and political issues at stake in these events.

Internal Pressures: Facing Fears

The progressive confrontations that *Good Night* re-creates suggest that beneath the courageous stances that made Murrow famous remained a need to face fear continually. One of Murrow's biographers writes of the journalist's perennial stage fright, both before the microphone as a radio correspondent, and also later, on television.[207] This, of course, would come at the end of whatever risks might have been involved, for example, in covering Nazi repression of dissidents in Berlin in the mid and late 1930s, or living under the bombs during the Blitz in 1940.[208] *Good Night* captures this sense of grappling with the causes and effects of inner pressure through the increasing tension in David Strathairn's performance of Murrow, and through, as is wholly necessary, Murrow's incessant smoking.

Strathairn's characterization conveys in every shot in the film the tautness evident in images of the actual Murrow. Archive footage from *See It Now* and *CBS Reports* programs makes widely available how Edward R. Murrow looked and sounded. To set this up, *Good Night* paints in brief, efficient strokes how *See It Now* as live television resulted from the tense interplay between the cutting room, where film from stories would be assembled and trimmed to fit the precise timing of a live broadcast, and the studio, where Murrow as anchor would coordinate his commentary and the rest of the program's materials. The increasing sense of risk within each of the programs we are seeing re-created only intensifies the baseline, pressure cooker atmosphere of real time television. All of it—the film's larger, progressive rhythm of confrontation, the legal, political, and professional risk-taking each program entails, set off by the frenetic activity of correspondents, crew, and technicians to bring it home in a live broadcast—funnels down as each program commences to Murrow in the anchor chair. Murrow faces all this with apparent implacability in contrast to the surrounding atmosphere of tremendous tension. Strathairn's realization of Murrow as performer, maintaining the same steady look, the same deliberate rhythm of speaking, the same short, clipped sentences that archive material has made so well known, becomes all the more credible as the contrast between steadfastness and surrounding turmoil gives us a sense of what this demeanor costs.

The other direct, visible indication of Murrow's driven nature is his smoking. Again, as biographies and archive material would indicate, Murrow's smoking is constant. A cigarette is evident in every scene, as it should be. Murrow's (in)famous smoking sets up one of the film's brief moments of dark humor, when he says to Friendly (George Clooney), who is lighting up the requisite cigarette for Murrow just before the McCarthy broadcast, "Funny thing, Freddie—every time you light a cigarette for me, I know you're lying." It is re-creation reminding us of its own limits. While a necessary link to the essence of the man Strathairn's performance evokes how images of the actual Murrow with his cigarettes allow us to watch self-extinction in slow motion, a suicide in small steps.

Another way *Good Night* conveys the interplay between external constraints and internal pressures is to depict Murrow throughout the film as a father figure. Murrow's need to defend victims is also evident close to home. We see him repeatedly asked to defend his beleaguered professional family, and these moments emphasize how he realizes, in asking each member of his team to join him in taking a moral stand, that it is their loyalty to Murrow that has made them vulnerable. The film shows the *See It Now* staff as a family, emphasizing how members of this surrogate family are potential victims of institutional repression because of the direction the program takes under Murrow's leadership. Murrow had established this kind of familial collegiality when he pulled together the "Murrow boys," the team of correspondents he coordinated in Europe during the war, and brought the same work patterns as well as many of the same workers into CBS television's news division.[209] *Good Night* shows Murrow's work family as a bulwark against a hostile, outer world. The studio scenes in the film invariably fall into familial configurations as the same group of colleagues discuss stories, review film, and prepare for broadcasts.

Good Night depicts in heroic, familial, melodramatic terms Murrow's desire to intercede for victims such as Radulovich and Moss, and to protect those working with him to use *See It Now* to effect necessary social change. The visible evidence we see re-created in the film of Murrow's need to face the sources of fear only suggests the larger fears that motivated Murrow, fears that potentially resonate with *Good Night, and Good Luck*'s contemporary audience. Before Murrow had covered Europe for CBS radio in the 1930s he worked to help relocate intellectuals and professionals attempting to flee Nazi repression.[210] The contacts and relationships he created in his committee work became a large part of his effectiveness as a journalist who covered European events in the mid and late 1930s. Murrow had direct, first-hand familiarity with the causes and consequences of fascist repression in Germany and Italy. Seeing similar tendencies in Joseph McCarthy's takeover of power in American politics had to provoke Murrow's greatest fear, that America would suffer from the same kind of cataclysm that he had witnessed devastate Europe. Certainly the parallels are striking: in the United States in the late 1940s and early 1950s, as in Germany in the 1930s, we see the progressive undermining of legitimate legal and political processes by a demagogic politician and his ardent followers; the persecution of dissent; the loss of livelihood for the dissenters; and a generally debilitating, suffocating atmosphere of fear and repression. Of all the inner demons motivating Murrow's need to confront the opposition, this particular pressure to perform to the utmost had to have been the strongest.

External Pressure: The Grain of the 50s

By placing its re-creation of Murrow's determined performance at its core, *Good Night* shows that the stands Murrow took in his broadcasts were courageous responses not only to inner pressures, but also to external threats. The film captures in several ways the all-pervasive pressure of the McCarthy era. The political, legal, and economic threats McCarthy's power wielded are evident in the film in the pressure put on Murrow by CBS management, and through the film's visual atmosphere.

The film re-creates the visual world of 1950s television in basic ways. Shot in black and white, *Good Night* emulates the contrast values of 1950s feature films and films shot for television programs.[211] The black and white documentary "look" dovetails with the actual documentary material *Good Night* incorporates from the *See It Now* archives. Cutting the archive material from the original broadcasts into the continuity of the re-creation warrants the claims the film is making, as a docudrama, as to what taking a stance through that broadcast at that particular moment in history must have been like.[212] The archive footage itself anchors these sequences squarely in the actuality the feature film re-creates. The difference in resolution between the feature's black and white stock, and the kinescopes it is re-presenting, creates part of what is essential to the film's visual grain, emphasizing the documentary nature of the original. The texture of the images ties the docudrama's re-creation to actuality.

Both kinds of material, archive and contemporary, are close-up intensive, evoking the personal, claustrophobic nature of the tensions surrounding the broadcasts, and the people responsible for them. At least two-thirds of *Good Night* is shot in medium close-up or closer. Often shots that begin framed as long shots or medium long shots zoom or track in to close-ups before the take is finished. The contracting of space in virtually every scene in the film, either through staging in the confines of the production studio or the shooting of the action, underlines the pressures the broadcasts and broadcasters were facing. As we see these characters in this relentlessly close proximity, the subject of virtually every conversation is pressure: will there be political backlash for what they are doing? Will sponsors and CBS corporate balk at the risk? Is taking what amounts to an editorial position in a news program professionally responsible and ethical?

The sense of claustrophobia pervades *Good Night*. One scene will suffice as an example, the moment prior to airing the Radulovich program. The lead-in establishes *See It Now*'s risk-taking broadcasts as especially tense moments within the already high-anxiety, frantic, down-to-the-wire atmosphere of live television that combined interviews and cut-aways on film with studio commentary. We alternate between the film editors trying to finish up, the production staff working elbow-to-elbow in the cramped control room, Murrow in place at a desk chair before a console, and

Friendly, crouching at Murrow's knee, ready to cue him to go on air. Space shrinks to the monitors, and Murrow in tight close-ups watching, and then commenting on the material. The contrast between the low resolution archive material, and denser grain, higher definition Murrow close-ups in the re-creation thrust us directly into the tension of advocacy.

The film's all-pervasive visual tightness echoes the personal, political, and social tension of the time, evoking in the largest sense the atmosphere of political repression in the United States in the 1950s. The film's visual style always returns to the tight shots of Murrow that frame his intransigence, his intractability. His stubborn, perhaps compulsive courage in the face of unimaginably huge pressures seems all the more necessary because the sense of external pressure is so ubiquitous in the film.

Good Night serves as an appropriate kind of cautionary tale for an audience learning more now of the (ab)use of political pressure to stifle dissent and circumvent the due process guaranteed by American law. At least indirectly the film reminds why, in 2005 and after, it would be necessary to have the courage to speak in a post-9/11 world, dominated by the Patriot Act and a president and vice-president who unhesitatingly attacked critics of administrative policy. Murrow's story is both exemplary and timely as it explains the cost of courage in the face of repressive political pressures. The explanation we see in *Good Night* of Murrow's courage in the face of internal and external constraints offers a timeless, necessary lesson in what it takes to speak truth to political power.

CHAPTER FIFTEEN

PERFORMING THE PAST: PRESENT AND FUTURE

Docudrama takes for its ongoing project the representation of the actual through the codes and conventions of classic Hollywood, feature film narrative form. If this means that, as it uses this form docudrama strives for a character-driven view of the actual, then more appropriate to what docudrama claims might be the reverse of this statement, that docudrama offers us an actuality-driven view of characters' ambitions, emotions, and compulsions. As actuality frames the character, conflict, and closure we find in Hollywood-style docudrama storytelling, the two recurring concerns the case studies here have developed become a clear implication of docudrama's balancing of documentary material and narrative representation (and the appeals inherent within that balance): first, setting anchors and informs docudrama's performance of the past, creating the reciprocal legibility of physical, social, and historical contexts, and the performance of what occurred within them. Story material in docudrama remains anchored to the actual. The process of reciprocal legibility in docudrama shapes public memory of events, war, and important lives as docudrama narrates them. Second, docudrama's performance of the past offers an opportunity to grasp the real through performance itself. Performing the past—performance anchored by the actual—becomes an opportunity to grasp the real by both stepping away from it (the "body too many" performance gives us) and at the same time, stepping into it by foregrounding how the actual anchors the performance we see.

Consequently in events docudramas what is public and known stages an individual work's performance of ambition. Events make personal ambition legible, whether it is political ambition (such as we see in films grappling with the resignation of Richard Nixon, the machinations of the Senate and the White House over the Supreme Court nomination process, or the political ambitions of the terrorists played out onboard United 93) or the ambitions enacted in work, as performed in *The Perfect Storm*, *Erin*

Brockovich, and *Pirates of Silicon Valley*. War docudramas of the last decade return to well-known events to perform the viscerality of combat so as to address, ironically, the meaning of war as mediated. Works such as *Uprising* and *Nuremberg* argue for the need to remember the Holocaust by recovering the emotions evoked by the unthinkable. Docudramas about recent armed conflicts argue that the performance of the visceral nature of combat can be a counterforce to the "game" mentality that distances officers and audiences from combat's reality. Working largely as cautionary tales, biopics argue that compulsive action is both the source and the cost of accomplishment.

Docudrama's performance of the past raises two final matters that future study of the mode should consider as they indicate the importance of performing the real for contemporary culture. Why do stars such as Russell Crowe and Denzel Washington have preferences for acting with facts? I'd like to suggest that stars who wish to prove that they are, in fact, actors, are attracted by the challenges of the arena. The arena, with its accompanying codes and the verdicts of its moral systems, becomes the measure of the strength of the performance. Further, the arena not only allows the fusion of actor and actuality, but also through the process of performing in the arena the actor becomes a participant in the ritual of recovering the past. The privilege for the performer is that the past is made present through their performance.

For similar reasons feature film docudramas appear in cycles; the opportunity to revisit arenas such as the events of 9/11 or the events of war addresses cultural needs related to identity and memory. The large number of war docudramas produced between 2000 and 2003 comes as no surprise. Why, however, were so many important biopics produced and distributed in the first half of the last decade? Further, why are so many of the subjects of recent biopics performers? As a group, the films not only examine the problem of fame, but also ask, what does accomplishment mean? What does it cost? What becomes "extraordinary" for a contemporary culture? Clearly the biopic offers a resonant means to recover the past within a culture that prefers performing the real. Re-creating noteworthy lives, like the work of re-creating important events, performs memory, performs the past, and gives us the opportunity to re-create ourselves.

BIBLIOGRAPHY

A Beautiful Mind. Dir. R. Howard. Universal, 2001.

A Might Heart. Dir. M. Winterbottom. Paramount, 2007.

Ambrose, Stephen E. *Band of Brothers: E Company, 506ᵗʰ Regiment, 101ˢᵗ Airborne from Normandy to Hitler's Eagle's Nest.* London: Pocket Books, 1992.

Amelia. Dir. M. Nair. Fox Searchlight, 2009.

Atkinson, Michael. "Patriot Shame." *The Village Voice,* March 6-12, 2002.

Band of Brothers. Prod. S. Spielberg, T. Hanks, et.al. HBO, 2001.

Baron, Cynthia and Sharon Carnicke. *Reframing Screen Performance.* Ann Arbor: University of Michigan Press, 2008.

Baron, Cynthia, Diane Carson, and Frank P. Tomasulo, eds. *More Than a Method: Trends and Traditions in Contemporary Film Performance.* Detroit: Wayne State University Press, 2004.

Barstow, David, and Robin Stein. "Under Bush, A New Age of Prepackaged News. *New York Times,* March 13, 2005, 1.

Black Hawk Down. Dir. R. Scott. Columbia, 2001.

Bloody Sunday. Dir. P. Greengrass. Paramount, 2002.

Bobby Jones: Stroke of Genius. Dir. R. Herrington. Dean River Productions, 2004.

Bowden, Mark. *Blackhawk Down: A Story of Modern War.* New York: New American Library, 1999.

Bradshaw, Peter. "Water Torture." *The Guardian (London)* July 28, 2000, 6.

Brook, Peter. *The Empty Space.* New York: Touchstone, 1968.

Burgoyne, Robert. *Film Nation: Hollywood Looks at U.S. History.* Minneapolis: University of Minnesota Press, 1997.

Burnham, Margaret A. "The Supreme Court Appointment Process and the Politics of Race and Sex," in Morrison, Toni, ed. *Race-ing Justice, Engendering Power: Essays on Anita Hill, Clarence Thomas, and the Construction of Social Reality.* NY: Pantheon, 1992, 290-322.

Butler, Judith. *Excitable Speech.* New York: Routledge, 1997.

Calhoun, John, "Horse Power." *American Cinematographer.* August 2003, 42-53.

Capote. Dir. B. Miller. A-Line, 2005.

Carr, David. "A Ringside Seat For Murrow vs. McCarthy." *New York Times.* September 14, 2005, 12; 26 (Arts).

Catch Me If You Can. Dir. S. Spielberg. DreamWorks SKG, 2002.

Changeling. Dir. C. Eastwood. Universal, 2008.

Cinderella Man. Dir. R. Howard. Universal, 2005.

Corliss, Richard. "*The Perfect Storm.*" *Time.* July 3, 2000, 56-57.

—. "Let's Roll." *Time.* April 17, 2006, 70-72.

Corner, John. *The Art of Record: A Critical Introduction to Documentary.* New York: Manchester University Press, 1996.

Corner, John. "Backward Looks: Mediating the Past." *Media Culture and Society* 28:3 (2006): 466-472.

Corner, John. "Performing the Real: Documentary Diversions," *Television and New Media* 3:3 (2002): 255-269.

Custen, George. *Bio/Pics: How Hollywood Constructed Public History.* New Brunswick: Rutgers University Press, 1992.

Dana, Will. "*Pirates of Silicon Valley,*" *Rolling Stone.* July 8-22, 1999, 161.

Dargis, Manohla. "Defiance Under Fire: Paul Greengrass's Harrowing 'United 93.' *New York Times.* April 28, 2006, http://movies.nytimes.com/2006/04/28/movies/28unit.html?scp=1&sq=dargis,%20united%2093&st=cse (accessed September 18, 2010).

Dawson, G. F. *Documentary Theatre in the United States: An Historical Survey and Analysis of Its Content, Form, and Stagecraft.* Westport: Greenwood Press, 1999.

Defiance. Dir. E. Zwick. Paramount, 2008.

Denby, David. "Horse Power." *The New Yorker,* August 4, 2003, 84-85.

Doherty, Thomas. "*Good Night and Good Luck.*" *Cineaste* 31 (Winter 2005): 53-58.

—. "The New War Movies as Moral Rearmament: *Black Hawk Down & We Were Soldiers.*" *Cineaste* 27:3 (2002): 4-8.

Douglas, Lawrence. "Film As Witness: Screening *Nazi Concentration Camps* Before the Nuremberg Tribunal." *The Yale Law Journal* 105: 449-81.

Dovey, Jon. *Freakshow: First Person Media and Factual Television.* London: Pluto Press, 2000.

Dowd, Maureen. "Liberties; Keep Your Shirt On!" *New York Times.* August 25, 1999, A:23.

Dujsik, M. "Beyond The Sea." http://mark-reviews-movies.tripod.com/reviews/B/beyondsea.htm (accessed September 10, 2010).

Ebbrecht, Tobias. "Docudramatizing History on TV: German and British Docudrama and Historical Event Television in the Memorial Year 2005." *European Journal of Cultural Studies* 10:1 (2007): 35-55.

—. "History, Public Memory and Media Event: Codes and Conventions of Historical Event-Television in Germany." *Media History* 13: 2/3 (2007): 221-234.

Ebert, Roger. "*United 93.*" *Chicago Sun Times.* April 28, 2006. http://rogerebert.suntimes.com/apps/pbcs.dll/article?AID=/20060427/R EVIEWS/60419006/1023 (accessed September 18, 2010).

Edgerton, Gary. "High Concept Small Screen." *Journal of Popular Film and Television* 19:3 (1991): 114-127.

Ellis, Jack. *The Documentary Idea.* Englewood Cliffs: Prentice-Hall, 1989.

Erin Brockovich. Dir. S. Soderbergh. Jersey Films, 2000.

Finding Neverland. Dir. M. Forster. Miramax, 2004.

Fisher, Bob, "If Wishes Were Horses." *ICB Magazine*, July 2003, 25-30.

Flags of Our Fathers. Dir. C. Eastwood. Dreamworks and Warner Bros., 2006.

Flax, Jane. *The American Dream in Black and White: The Clarence Thomas Hearings.* Ithaca: Cornell University Press, 1998.

French, Philip. "The Price of Fish." *The Observer.* July 30, 2000, 9.

Fries, Laura. "*Strange Justice.*" *Daily Variety.* August 27, 1999.

Frost/Nixon. Dir. R. Howard. Universal, 2009.

Gilbert, Matthew. "*Strange Justice* Spins Different View." *Boston Globe*, August 27, 1999. E1.

Goffman, Erving. *The Presentation of Self in Everyday Life.* New York: Penguin, 1969.

—. *Frame Analysis.* New York: Harper & Row, 1974.

Goldman, Michael. "Making History." *Millimeter.* November-December 2008, 10.

Good Night, and Good Luck. Dir. G. Clooney. Warner Independent Pictures, 2005.

Great Debaters, The. Dir. D. Washington. Harpo Films, 2007.

Hariman, Robert and John Louis Locaites. *No Caption Needed: Iconic Photographs, Public Culture, and Liberal Democracy.* Chicago: University of Chicago Press, 2007.

Harris, Lyle V. "Story Embellishments Turn Justice Strange." *Atlanta Constitution.* August 27, 1999, 4F.

Harrop, John. *Acting.* London: Routledge, 1992.

Hazen, Don, "The Right Wing Express." *Alternet.* February 7, 2005. http://www.alternet.org/story/21192/ (accessed September 18, 2010).

Hidalgo. Dir. J. Johnston. Touchstone, 2004.

Hill, Michael E. "Showtime's *Strange Justice.*" *Washington Post,* August 29, 1999, Y04.

Hillenbrand, Laura. *Seabiscuit: An American Legend.* New York: Ballantine Books, 2001.

Himmelstein, M.Y. *Drama Was a Weapon.* Newark: Rutgers University Press, 1963.

Hirsch, Joshua. "Posttraumatic Cinema and the Holocaust Documentary." *Film & History* 32:1 (2002): 9-20.

Hoerschelmann, Olaf. "*Memoria Dextera Est*: Film and Public Memory in Postwar Germany." *Cinema Journal* 40:2 (2001): 78-97.

Hukill, Traci, "Seabiscuit's Joyride," *Alternet.* July 31, 2003. http://www.alternet.org/story/16514/seabiscuit%27s_joyride/ (accessed September 18, 2010).

James, Caryn. "He Said, She Said, and the Whole Nation Listened." *New York Times.* August. 27, 1999, E:29.

Johnson, Brian D. "*The Perfect Storm.*" *Maclean's.* July 10, 2000, 51-52.

Junger, Sebastian. "Watching Hollywood Brew a 'Perfect Storm.'" *New York Times.* April 30, 2000, 4; 14.

Klawans, Stuart. "*The Perfect Storm.*" *The Nation.* July 24-31, 2000, 43-44.

Krantz, Michael. "The Way They Were." *Time.* June 14, 1999, 222.

Lacour, Claudia Brodsky. "Doing Things With Words: 'Racism' as Speech act and the Undoing of Justice," in Morrison, Toni, ed. *Race-ing Justice, En-gendering Power: Essays on Anita Hill, Clarence Thomas, and the Construction of Social Reality.* New York: Pantheon, 1992, 127-158.

Landsberg, Allison. *Prosthetic Memory: The Transformation of American Remembrance in the Age of Mass Culture.* New York: Columbia University Press, 2004.

LaSalle, Mick. "Jamie Foxx Plays It just Right." *San Francisco Chronicle.* October 29, 2004. http://www.sfgate.com/cgi-bin/article. cgi?f=/c/a/2004/10/29/DDGDD9HHM017.DTL. (accessed September 18, 2010).

Leab, Daniel. "The Moving Image As Interpreter of History: Telling the Dancer from the Dance." John O'Connor, ed. *Image as Artifact: The Historical Analysis of Film and Television.* Malabar, Florida: Krieger, 1990.

Lipkin, Steven N. *Real Emotional Logic: Film and Television Docudrama as Persuasive Practice.* Carbondale: Southern Illinois University Press, 2002.

Lipton, Mike. *"Pirates of Silicon Valley." People Weekly.* June 21, 1999, 27.

Longman, Jere. "Paul Greengrass's Filming of Flight 93's Story, Trying to Define Heroics." *New York Times*, April 24, 2006, http://www.nytimes.com/2006/04/24/movies/24unit.html?_r=1&scp=1 0&sq=united%2093&st=cse. (accessed September 18, 2010).

Lopate, Phillip. *Film Comment* 41 (Sep./Oct. 2005): 30-34, 37.

Lubiano, Wahneema. "Black Ladies, Welfare Queens, and State Minstrels: Ideological War by Narrative Means," in Morrison, Toni, ed. *Race-ing Justice, En-gendering Power: Essays on Anita Hill, Clarence Thomas, and the Construction of Social Reality.* New York: Pantheon, 1992, 323-361.

MacDonald, Andrew and Gina. "Writing the Storm: Interview with Bill Whitliff." *Creative Screenwriting.* July-August 2000, 67-73.

Marable, Manning. "Clarence Thomas and the Crisis of Black Political Culture," in Morrison, Toni, ed. *Race-ing Justice, En-gendering Power: Essays on Anita Hill, Clarence Thomas, and the Construction of Social Reality.* NY: Pantheon, 1992, 61-85.

Marcks, Greg. "A Credible Witness." *Film Quarterly* 60:1 (Fall 2006): 3.

Marks, Laura. *The Skin of the Film: Intercultural Cinema, Embodiment, and the Senses.* Durham: Duke University Press, 2000.

Mason, G. "Documentary Drama From the Revue to the Tribunal." *Modern Drama* 20 (1977): 262-277.

Massing, Michael. "Black Hawk Downer." *The Nation.* February 25, 2002.

Mayer, Jane, and Jill Abramson. *Strange Justice: The Selling of Clarence Thomas.* New York: Houghton Mifflin, 1994.

McCarthy, Todd. *"Defiance." Variety.* November 17-23, 2008, 31.

Milk. Dir. G. Van Sant. Focus Features, 2008.

Miller, Anita. *The Complete Transcripts of the Clarence Thomas—Anita Hill Hearings October 11, 12, 13, 1991.* Chicago: Academy Chicago Publishers, 1994.

Mink, Eric. "Doing 'Justice' To History: Hill-Thomas Telefilm Alters Facts But Finds the Dramatic Essence." *Daily News*, August 27, 1999, 135.

Moore, Frazier. *"Strange Justice* Revisits Divisive Debate." *Dayton Daily News*, August 29, 1999.

Moore, Harold G. and Joseph L. Galloway, *We Were Soldiers Once ... and Young.* New York: Random House, 1992.

Morrison, Toni, "Introduction: Friday on the Potomac," in Morrison, Toni, ed. *Race-ing Justice, En-gendering Power: Essays on Anita*

Hill, Clarence Thomas, and the Construction of Social Reality. New York: Pantheon, 1992, vi-xxx.

Munich. Dir. S. Spielberg. DreamWorks SKG, 2005.

Naremore, James. *Acting in the Cinema.* Berkeley: University of California Press, 1988.

Nichols, Bill. *Representing Reality.* Bloomington: Illinois University Press, 1991.

Nixon. Dir. O. Stone. Cinergi Pictures, 1995.

Nuremberg. Dir. Y. Simoneau. Alliance/Atlantis Communications, 2000.

O'Connor, J. and L. Brown. *The Federal Theatre Project.* London: Methuen, 1980.

O'Hagan, Andrew. "Bad Weather Report for George Clooney." *The Daily Telegraph (London).* July 28, 2000, 23.

O'Reilly, Basha and CuChullaine, eds. *Hidalgo and Other Stories by Frank T. Hopkins.* Geneva, Switzerland: The Long Riders' Guild Press, 2003.

Orgeron, Marsha. 'The Most Profound Shock': Traces of the Holocaust in Samuel Fuller's *Verboten!* (1955) and *The Big Red One* (1980). *Historical Journal of Film, Radio and Television* 27:4(2007): 471-511.

Paget, Derek. *No Other Way To Tell It: Dramadoc/Docudrama on Television.* Manchester and New York: Manchester University Press, 1998.

—. *True Stories?: Documentary Drama on Radio, Stage and Screen.* Manchester and New York: Manchester University Press, 1990.

Persico, Joseph E. *Edward R. Murrow.* New York: McGraw-Hill, 1988.

Persico, Joseph. *Nuremberg: Infamy on Trial.* New York: Viking, 1994.

Phillips, Kendall R. ed. *Framing Public Memory.* Tuscaloosa: University of Alabama Press, 2004.

Pirates of Silicon Valley. Dir. M. Burke. TNT, 1999.

Rapaport, Lynn. "Hollywood's Holocaust: *Schindler's List* and the Construction of Memory." *Film & History* 32:1 (2002), 55-65.

Ray. Dir. T. Hackford. Universal, 2004.

Renov, Michael, ed. *Theorizing Documentary.* New York: Routledge, 1993.

Rich, Frank. "Enron: Patron Saint of Bush's Fake News." *New York Times.* March 20, 2005, sec. 2:1+.

Rokem, Freddie. *Performing History: Theatrical Representations of the Past in Contemporary Theatre.* Iowa City: University of Iowa Press, 2000.

Rosenstone, Robert, *Visions of the Past.* Cambridge: Harvard University Press, 1995.

—. *History On Film/Film On History*. Harlow, UK: Pearson, 2006.

—. *Revisioning History*. Princeton: Princeton University Press, 1995.

Rosenthal, Alan, ed. *Why Docudrama?* Carbondale: Southern Illinois University Press, 1999.

Rozen, Leah. "*The Perfect Storm*." *People Weekly*. July 10, 2000, 37.

Saving Jessica Lynch. Dir. P. Markle. NBC, 2003.

Schatz, Thomas. *Hollywood Genres*. New York: Random House, 1981.

Schwartz, Missy. "Ready or Not." *Entertainment Weekly* 874/875, April 28, 2006-May 5, 2006, 13-14.

Scott, A.O. "Early in the Vietnam War, on an Ill-Defined Mission." *New York Times*. March 1, 2002.

—. "Here's To Postwar America, We Never Really Knew Ye." *New York Times*. December 4, 2005: 24 (Arts).

Seabiscuit. Dir. G. Ross. Universal, 2003.

Secret Honor. Dir. R. Altman. Sandcastle 5 Productions, 1984.

Simon, John. "*The Perfect Storm*." *National Review*. July 31, 2000: 50-51.

Smiley, Jane. *A Year At the Races*. New York: Alfred Knopf, 2004.

Smith Gavin. "Mission Statement." *Film Comment* 42:3 (May/June 2006): 25.

Sperber, A. M. *Murrow: His Life and Times*. New York: Freundlich Books, 1986.

Staiger, Janet. *Perverse Spectators: The Practice of Film Reception*. New York: New York University Press, 2000.

Stanislavski, Constantin. *An Actor Prepares*. Elizabeth Hapgood, trans. London: Geoffrey Bles, 1955.

"*Strange Justice* Favours Anita Hill." *Calgary Herald*. August 23, 1999, B6.

Strange Justice. Dir. E. Dickerson. Paramount, 1999.

Strasberg, Lee and Evangeline Morpbos. *A Dream of Passion: The Development of the Method*. Boston: Little Brown, 1987.

Strong, Phil. *Horses and America*. New York: Frederick A. Stokes, 1939.

Szaloky, Melinda. "Sounding Images in Silent Film: Visual Acoustics in Murnau's *Sunrise*. *Cinema Journal* 41:2 (2002): 109-131.

Taylor, C. (2004) "Ray." salon.com 29 Oct. 2004. http://www.salon.com/entertainment/movies/review/2004/10/29/ray (accessed September 18, 2010).

Taylor, Telford. *The Anatomy of the Nuremberg Trials*. New York: Alfred A. Knopf, 1992.

The Aviator. Dir. M. Scorcese. Warner Bros., 2004.

The Greatest Game Ever Played. Dir. B. Paxton. Disney, 2005.

The Perfect Storm. Dir. W. Peterson. Warner Bros., 2000.

The Pianist. Dir. R. Polanski. Universal, 2002.

Thomas, Kendall. "Strange Fruit," in Morrison, Toni, ed. *Race-ing Justice, En-gendering Power: Essays on Anita Hill, Clarence Thomas, and the Construction of Social Reality.* New York: Pantheon, 1992, 364-389.

Thompson, Kevin D. "Thomas vs. Hill: The Drama of *Strange Justice.*" *Palm Beach Post.* August 29, 1999, 1J.

Timmons, Heather. "Four Years On, A Cabin's Eye View of 9/11." *New York Times*, January 1, 2006, AR 7; 22.

Turan, Kenneth. "United 93." *Los Angeles Times.* April 28, 2006. http://www.calendarlive.com/movies/turan/cl-et-united28apr28,0,795 6334.story (accessed September 18, 2010).

United 93. Dir. P. Greengrass. Universal, 2006.

Uprising. Dir. J.Avnet. Avnet/Kerner Production, 2001.

Walk the Line. Dir. J. Mangold. Fox 2000 Pictures, 2005.

Walker, Janet. *Trauma Cinema: Documenting Incest and the Holocaust.* Berkeley: University of California Press, 2005.

We Were Soldiers. Dir. R. Wallace. Paramount, 2002.

Weinraub, Bernard. "Hill vs. Thomas, Again in the Court of Senate Opinion." *New York Times.* August 22, 1999, sec. 2:31.

Weiss, Peter. "The Material and the Models: Notes Towards A Definition of Documentary Theatre." *Theatre Quarterly* 1 (1971): 41-43.

White, Hayden. *The Content of the Form.* Baltimore: Johns Hopkins University Press, 1989.

World Trade Center. Dir. O. Stone. Paramount, 2006.

Wright, Will. *Six Guns and Society: A Structural Study of the Western.* Los Angeles: University of California Press, 1975.

Zacharek, Stephanie. "United 93." *Salon.com.* April 28, 2006, http://www.salon.com/ent/movie/review/2006/04/26/united_93 (accessed September 10, 2010).

NOTES

[1] Interview with the author, March 24, 2010.

[2] Steven N. Lipkin, *Real Emotional Logic: Film and Television Docudrama as Persuasive Practice* (Carbondale: Southern Illinois University Press, 2002).

[3] Recent work in film genre has built upon the foundations in genre theory developed since the 1980s by scholars such as: Thomas Schatz in *Hollywood Genres* (New York: Random House, 1981); Nick Browne in *Refiguring American Film Genres* (Berkeley: University of California Press, 1998); Rick Altman's "A Semantic/Syntactic Approach to Film Genre" in Leo Braudy, ed., *Film Theory and Criticism* (New York: Oxford University Press, 2004): 680-690; and Steve Neale, *Genre and Hollywood* (New York: Routledge, 2000).

[4] John Belton, *American Cinema/American Culture*, 2d ed. (Boston: McGraw Hill, 2005), 133. Belton implies that a mode is an "attitude or method of treatment." (134)

[5] Nichols writes: "Modes are something like genres, but instead of coexisting as different types of imaginary worlds ... modes represent different concepts of historical representation." Bill Nichols, *Representing Reality* (Bloomington: University of Indiana Press, 1991), 23.

[6] Lipkin, *Logic,* 4.

[7] John Corner, "Performing the Real: Documentary Diversions," *Television and New Media* 3:3 (2002): 255-269.

[8] Nichols is discussing how re-creation provides "one body too many" in the form of the actor; see *Representing Reality,* 249-250.

[9] Lipkin, *Logic,* 5; 13.

[10] Chapter Three in *Reframing* opens by stating: "The dense array of connotatively rich gestures, postures, intonations, and inflections seen and heard in film are the material, intratextual elements that belong to filmic representation in the same way that lighting design and editing patterns do. Importantly, performance details contribute to the flow of narrative information, interpretation about characters' desires, their confrontations, and their choices depend in part on the sense that audience members make of actors' gestures and expressions." Cynthia Baron and Sharon Carnicke, *Reframing Screen Performance* (Ann Arbor: University of Michigan Press, 2008), 62.

[11] See in particular Part II ("Performance Elements, Cinematic Connections, and Cultural Traditions") with instructive analyses of Chaplin's *City Lights,* adaptations of *Romeo and Juliet* and *Hamlet,* and a comparison of *The Seven Samurai* and *The Magnificent Seven.*

[12] Tomasulo in Cynthia Baron, Diane Carson, and Frank Tomasulo, eds., *More than A Method: Trends and Traditions in Contemporary Film Performance* (Detroit: Wayne State University Press, 2004), 96.

[13] Diane Carson, "Plain and Simple: Masculinity Through John Sayles's Lens," (173-191); pages 183-184 are particularly helpful here.

[14] Paul MacDonald, "Why Study Film Acting? Some Opening Reflections" in Baron, Carson, and Tomasulo's *More Than a Method* (39) offers more on acting techniques that serve and are served by cognitive and emotional point of view strategies.

[15] See, for example, essays in Kendall R. Phillips, ed., *Framing Public Memory* (Tuscaloosa: University of Alabama Press, 2004); Allison Landsberg, *Prosthetic Memory: The Transformation of American Remembrance in the Age of Mass Culture* (New York: Columbia University Press, 2004); and Olaf Hoerschelmann, "*Memoria Dextera Est*: Film and Public Memory in Postwar Germany," *Cinema Journal* 40:2 (2001): 78-97.

[16] Interview with the author, October 14, 2009.

[17] Sociologist Erving Goffman has termed as "frames" the interrelationship between setting and role. He notes: "The nature of a particular frame will, of course, be linked to the nature of the person-role formula it sustains ... no matter where on this continuum a particular formula is located, the formula itself will express the sense in which the framed activity is geared into the continuing world." Erving Goffman, *Frame Analysis* (New York: Harper & Row, 1974), 269.

[18] The entire Spring/Summer 2006 issue of *Journal of Film and Video* explores the carryover of theatrical theories of acting into film. In this collection Philip Drake's "Reconceptualizing Screen Performance" is particularly helpful in exploring how various coding systems that frame performance in film affect the legibility of performance on screen (see p. 81). See also Baron, Carson, and Tomasulo, eds., *More than A Method*.

[19] Lipkin, *Logic*, 12-31.

[20] Tom Schatz has suggested a similar idea in distinguishing between genres of determinate and indeterminate space. "Determinate" space sets action in within ideologically contested settings that provide "an arena for conflicts, which are themselves determined by the actions and attitudes of the participants." Schatz, *Hollywood Genres*, 24-25.

[21] Robert Rosenstone, *History On Film/Film On History* (Harlow, UK: Pearson, 2006), 31.

[22] The power of cultural icons to shape public memory has been explored through an in-depth, case study approach by Robert Hariman and John Louis Locaites in *No Caption Needed: Iconic Photographs, Public Culture, and Liberal Democracy* (Chicago: University of Chicago Press, 2007). Within their chapter on the iconographic evolution of the photograph of the flag raising on Mt. Suribachi, they suggest that the photo, as a "model of civic identity" (95) contributes to a sense of national identity through its image of civic performance. (See "Performing Civic Identity," ibid., 93-136).

[23] Brian D. Johnson, "*The Perfect Storm*," *Maclean's*, July 2000, 51-52.

[24] Richard Corliss, "*The Perfect Storm*," *Time*, July 3, 2000, 56-57.

[25] Peter Bradshaw, "Water Torture," *The Guardian*, July 28, 2000, 6.

[26] Stuart Klawans, "*The Perfect Storm*," *The Nation*, July 24-31, 2000, 43-44.

[27] John Simon, *"The Perfect Storm," National Review*, July 31, 2000, 50-51.

[28] See Corliss, Johnson, and Bradshaw; also see Andrew O'Hagan, "Bad Weather Report for George Clooney," *The Daily Telegraph (London)*, July 28, 2000, 23.

[29] Ibid.

[30] Johnson, *"Storm,"* 51-52.

[31] Leah Rozen, *"The Perfect Storm," People Weekly*, July 10, 2000, 37.

[32] Bradshaw, "Torture," 6.

[33] Klawans, "Storm," 43-44.

[34] Ibid.

[35] Philip French, "The Price of Fish," *The Observer*, July 30, 2000, 9.

[36] Ibid.

[37] Corliss, "Perfect Storm," 56-57.

[38] Andrew and Gina MacDonald, "Writing the Storm: Interview With Bill Whitliff," *Creative Screenwriting*, July-August 2000, 69-70.

[39] Sebastian Junger, "Watching Hollywood Brew a Perfect Storm," *New York Times*, April 30, 2000, Arts, 4.

[40] Janet Staiger, *Perverse Spectators: The Practice of Film Reception* (New York: New York University Press, 2000), 5.

[41] Ibid., 198.

[42] Philip French, "A Woman's Gotta Do," *The Observer*, April 9, 2000, 9.

[43] Tom Doherty, *"Erin Brockovich," Cineaste* 25 (2000): 40-41.

[44] B.D. Johnson, *"Erin Brockovich," Maclean's*, March 20, 2000, 71; Stanley Kauffman, *"Erin Brockovich," The New Republic*, April 3, 2000, 24; and Stuart Klawans, *"Erin Brockovich," The Nation*, April 10, 2000, 32-36.

[45] In 1999 alone, works included *A Civil Action* (S. Zaillan), *At First Sight* (I. Winkler), *Hilary and Jackie* (A. Tucker), *October Sky* (J. Johnston), *Patch Adams* (T. Shadyac), *Music of the Heart* (W. Craven), *The Insider* (M. Mann) and *The Hurricane* (N. Jewison).

[46] Klawans, *"Brockovich,"* 32-36.

[47] Doherty, *"Brockovich,"* 40-41.

[48] Staiger, *Spectators,* 198.

[49] C. Booth, *"Erin Brockovich," Time*, May 1, 2000, 70.

[50] Interview with the author, October 14, 2009.

[51] Derek Paget's seminal work on docudrama on British television is titled appropriately *No Other Way To Tell It: Dramadoc/docudrama On Television* (Manchester: Manchester University Press, 1998).

[52] Gary Edgerton, "High Concept Small Screen," *Journal of Popular Film and Television* 19:3 (1991): 118.

[53] Douglas Gomery, *"Brian's Song*: Television, Hollywood, and the Evolution of the Movie Made For Television." *Television: The Critical View,* Horace Newcombe, ed., 4th ed. *(*New York: Oxford University Press, 1987), 213.

[54] Todd Gitlin, *Inside Prime Time* (New York: Pantheon, 1983), 164.

[55] Interview with the author. Burke said also: "It is "one of the more Shakespearean dramas in public life. You have everything—ambition, lust, greed, betrayal" since we see Jobs in particular as "the most Shakespearean character in

American public life, a man with enormous personal problems that coincided with his rise and fall at Apple in very grand ways."
[56] Of this moment writer/director Burke says: "if you're writing about something that's absolutely happened that was not fiction, it could be implausible, but if it happened, it happened.   So that's a dramatic defense for using things.   For instance, there's a scene in there where Steve Jobs is talking to a prospective employee. He is actually interviewing a guy who wanted to go work for Apple. And he puts his bare feet on the desk and kind of frames the guy's face with his bare feet. He acts in a really hostile way. That actually happened." Interview with the author.
[57] Will Dana, *"Pirates of Silicon Valley," Rolling Stone*, July 8-22, 1999, 161; Mike Lipton, *"Pirates of Silicon Valley," People Weekly*, June 21, 1999, 27; and Michael Krantz, "The Way They Were," *Time*, June 14, 1999, 222.
[58] Staiger, *Spectators,* 197.
[59] Ibid., 198.
[60] Basha O'Reilly, *Hidalgo and Other Stories by Frank T. Hopkins* (Geneva, Switzerland: The Long Riders' Guild Press, 2003), 2-12 and subsequently, provides a thorough examination of the historical bases of Hopkins's claims. This research dismisses most of them, including disputing the very existence of the 3000 mile Arabian race.
[61] Will Wright, *Six Guns and Society: A Structural Study of the Western* (Los Angeles: University of California Press, 1975), 189-190.
[62] Phil Strong, *Horses and America* (New York: Frederick A. Stokes, 1939), 76.
[63] Wright, *Six Guns*, 50.
[64] Marshall McLuhan, *Understanding Media: The Extensions of Man* (New York: McGraw-Hill, 1965), 22-32.
[65] Wright, *Six Guns, 142.*
[66] Jane Smiley, *A Year At the Races* (New York: Alfred Knopf, 2004), 6.
[67] Strong, *Horses*, 163.
[68] What follows includes:

> We never know how high we are
> Till we are called to rise;
> And then, if we are true to plan,
> Our statures touch the skies.
>
> The heroism we recite
> Would be a daily thing,
> Did not ourselves the cubits warp
> For fear to be a king.

Emily Dickinson, *Complete Poems*, http://www.bartleby.com/113/1097.html.
[69] Writing in *The New Yorker*, David Denby took issue with this particular strategy in the film: "McCullough's narration—liberal and humane, witty but not sarcastic, knowing but not clever—is an ideal voice for a documentary, but it's wrong for a

narrative film. It argues for the rightness, the sanity of its own intelligently rueful point of view—it's like a seal of approval. Why wasn't Ross content to just let the movie make the point? We can see for ourselves that thousands of destitute people adore the come-from-behind animal. The overexplicitness is a form of special pleading—Ross borrows the high authority of PBS rather than achieving something better through dramatic representation." David Denby, "Horse Power," *The New Yorker,* August 4, 2003, 85.

[70] See http://www.imdb.com/title/tt0192634/ regarding Rupert Murdoch's role in Fox's abandonment of the production.

[71] See, for example, Frank Rich, "Enron: Patron Saint of Bush's Fake News," *New York Times,* March 20, 2005, sec. 2, 1; and David Barstow, and Robin Stein, "Under Bush: A New Age of Prepackaged News," *New York Times,* March 13, 2005, 1.

[72] Jane Mayer and Jill Abramson, *Strange Justice: The Selling of Clarence Thomas (*New York: Houghton Mifflin, 1994), 13; 152-153.

[73] Ibid., 175; 191-192; 196; also Manning Marable, "Clarence Thomas and the Crisis of Black Political Culture," in Toni Morrison, ed, *Race-ing Justice, Engendering Power: Essays on Anita Hill, Clarence Thomas, and the Construction of Social Reality* (New York: Pantheon, 1992), 72-73.

[74] Don Hazen, "The Right Wing Express," *Alternet,* February 7, 2005, http://www.alternet.org/story/21192/.

[75] According to Margaret A. Burnham, the process of mobilizing campaigns by national political interests to influence Federal court nominations began with the battle over Robert Bork. See Margaret A. Burnham, "The Supreme Court Appointment Process and Politics of Race and Sex," in Morrison, *Race-ing Justice,* 292.

[76] Marable, "Crisis," 61-63, and Mayer, *Justice,*" 18-19; 53.

[77] Mayer, *Justice,* 21.

[78] Ibid., 162.

[79] Hill narrates in detail her experience of the Thomas nomination and hearing process in Anita Hill, *Speaking Truth to Power* (New York: Doubleday, 1997) with a view to analyzing the responses of individual senators on the Judiciary Committee and others to her charges. She discusses the hearing itself as a process of constructing narratives in "Marriage and Patronage in the Empowerment and Disempowerment of African American Women (273-4) in Anita Faye Hill and Emma Coleman Jordan, eds., *Race, Gender, and Power in America: The Legacy of the Hill-Thomas Hearings* (New York: Oxford University Press, 1995), 271-291.

[80] See also Morrison, *Race-ing,* xviii-xix.

[81] Jane Flax, *The American Dream in Black and White: The Clarence Thomas Hearings* (Ithaca: Cornell University Press, 1998), 50.

[82] For an analysis of this pronouncement as speech act, see Claudia B. Lacour, "Doing Things With Words: 'Racism' As Speech Act and the Undoing of Justice," Morrison, *Race-ing,* 151; and Kendall Thomas, "Strange Fruit," Ibid., 364-372; see also Lacour's discussion of victimization here as scapegoating (Ibid.,

151); for a discussion of racial roles and stereotyping in the larger Hill/Thomas discourse, see Wahneema Lubiano, "Black Ladies, Welfare Queens, and State Minstrels: Ideological War By Narrative Means," Morrison, *Race-ing*, 323-361.
[83] Kevin D. Thompson, "Thomas vs. Hill: The Drama of *Strange Justice*," *Palm Beach Post*, August 29, 1999, 1J; Michael E. Hill, "Showtime's *Strange Justice*," *Washington Post*, August 29, 1999, Y04; Eric Mink, "Doing 'Justice' To History: Hill-Thomas Telefilm Alters Facts But Finds the Dramatic Essence," *Daily News*, August 27, 1999, 135; and Caryn James, "He Said, She Said, and the Whole Nation Listened," *New York Times*, August 27, 1999, sec. E, 29.
[84] Elsewhere I have discussed "interaction" as a warranting strategy characteristic of docudrama. Interaction strategies pull together actual and staged scene elements to warrant the validity of docudramatic re-creation. See Lipkin, *Logic*, 25-27.
[85] In their description of this moment, Mayer and Abramson add the following: "Originally such speculation would be considered so prejudicial that it would never be allowed in an open court, let alone a Senate hearing. But that Saturday, the Republicans on the Judiciary Committee read portions from both *The Exorcist* and the 10th Circuit case out loud. Duberstein even told Hatch to hold up a copy of the book when questioning Thomas, on the theory that photos of the incriminating moment would run on the front page of every newspaper the following morning." Mayer, *Justice*, 302.
[86] Anita Miller, *The Complete Transcripts of the Clarence Thomas-Anita Hill Hearings October 11, 12, 13, 1991* (Chicago: Academy Chicago Publishers, 1994), 161.
[87] Ibid., 117.
[88] Ibid., 117-118.
[89] See, for example, David E. Rosenbaum and Lynette Clemetson, "In Fight to Confirm New Justice, Two Field Generals Rally Their Troops Again," *New York Times*, July 3, 2005, 15; and Matt Bai, "The Framing Wars," *The New York Times Magazine*, July 17, 2005, 38-45.
[90] Interview with the author, November 23, 2009.
[91] Lipkin, *Logic*, 47-54.
[92] For discussion of the defining characteristics of docudrama as a hybrid mode of representation see Lipkin, *Logic*, 1-11.
[93] Many are referenced in my discussion of *JFK* (Lipkin, *Logic*, 47-50). For a sampling of the discourse surrounding *Schindler's List*, see Yosefa Loshitzky, ed., *Spielberg's Holocaust: Critical Perspectives on Schindler's List* (Bloomington: Indiana University Press, 1997).
[94] According to the NBC *Evening News*, January 2, 2007, YouTube reported more than 1 million hits on its link to the Hussein video.
[95] More discussions of the film's production appear in Missy Schwartz, "Ready or Not," *Entertainment Weekly* 874/875, April 28, 2006-May 5, 2006, 13-14, as well as articles by Richard Corliss, "Let's Roll," *Time* 16, April 17, 2006, 70-72; Heather Timmons, "Four Years On, A Cabin's Eye View of 9/11" *New York Times*, January 1, 2006, AR 7; 22; and Kenneth Turan, "*United 93*," *Los Angeles*

Times, April 28, 2006, http://www.calendarlive.com/movies/turan/cl-et-united28ap
r28,0,7956334.story.

[96] Roger Ebert, *"United 93," Chicago Sun Times*, April 28, 2006,
http://rogerebert.suntimes.com/apps/pbcs.dll/article?AID=/20060427/REVIEWS/6
0419006/1023; Turan, *"United 93."*

[97] See Turan, *"United 93,"* for example, for some comparison of Greengrass's
approach here to the work of Humphrey Jennings. See Pavlus for comparison to
the methods of Ken Loach (in John Pavlus, "A Doomed Flight and a Broken
Romance." *American Cinematographer,* June 2006, 26-30).

[98] Greg Marcks, "A Credible Witness," *Film Quarterly* 60:1 (Fall 2006): 3.

[99] Gavin Smith, "Mission Statement," *Film Comment* 42:3 (May/June 2006): 25.

[100] The hijackers' names, as I identify them here through their functions, are: pilot:
Ziad Jarrah; copilot: Ahmad Al Nami; instigator: Saeed al Ghamdi; bomber:
Ahmad al Haznami. See *The 9/11 Commission Report* (New York: W. W.
Norton, Inc., 2004), p. 4.

[101] Sandra Bradshaw, played by Trish Gates, a United Air Lines flight attendant.

[102] Mark Bingham, played by Cheyenne Jackson.

[103] Thomas Burnett, played by Christian Clemenson.

[104] See Longman (Jere Longman, "Paul Greengrass's Filming of Flight 93's Story,
Trying to Define Heroics." *New York Times*, April 24, 2006,
http://www.nytimes.com/2006/04/24/movies/24unit.html?_r=1&scp=10&sq=unite
d%2093&st=cse) for some discussion of the film's approach to the problem of the
political discourse of the time exploiting passenger heroics.

[105] *The 9/11 Commission Report*, p. 31; Peter Bradshaw, *"United 93," Guardian
Unlimited*, June 2, 2006, http://www.guardian.co.uk/culture/2006/jun/02/1.

[106] Manohla Dargis, "Defiance Under Fire: Paul Greengrass's Harrowing 'United
93,' *New York Times*, April 28, 2006,
http://movies.nytimes.com/2006/04/28/movies/28unit.html?scp=1&sq=dargis,%20
united%2093&st=cse); Turan, *"United 93;"* Stephanie Zacharek, *"United 93,"*
Salon.com, April 28, 2006,
http://www.salon.com/ent/moview/review/2006/04/26/united_93

[107] Allison Landsberg has termed this kind of mediated, secondary memory as
"prosthetic memory." See Landsberg, *Prosthetic Memory,* 4.

[108] Janet Walker, *Trauma Cinema: Documenting Incest and the Holocaust*
(Berkeley: University of California Press, 2005), 19.

[109] Ibid.

[110] Joshua Hirsh, "Posttraumatic Cinema and the Holocaust Documentary," *Film
& History* 32: 1 (2002): 9-20.

[111] Ibid, 11.

[112] Hirsch, "Posttraumatic Cinema" writes: "Documentary images must be
submitted to a narrative discourse the purpose of which is, if not to literally
traumatize the spectator, at least to invoke a posttraumatic historical consciousness—
a kind of textual compromise between the senselessness of the initial traumatic
encounter and the sense-making apparatus of a fully integrated historical narrative
…" (11) This is necessary because: "As trauma is less a particular experiential

content than a *form* of experience, also the discourse of trauma in this second phase is defined less by a particular image content than by the attempt to discover a form for presenting the content that mimics some aspects of PTSD itself—the attempt to formally reproduce for the spectator an experience of once again suddenly seeing the unthinkable. And insofar as what is historically thinkable is partly constituted by the conventions of the historical film genre, the instigation of a cinematic discourse of trauma becomes a question of upsetting the spectator's expectations not only of history in general, but also of the historical film in particular." (11-12)

[113] Ibid, 12.

[114] Todd McCarthy, "*Defiance,*" *Variety,* November 17-23, 2008, 31.

[115] Michael Goldman, "Making History," *Millimeter,* November-December 2008, 10.

[116] Landsberg sees the media as the main operating theater for the attachment of such prostheses. Landsberg states: "Modernity makes possible and necessary a new form of public cultural memory. This new form of memory, which I call prosthetic memory, emerges at the interface between a person and a historical narrative about the past, at an experiential site such as a movie theater or museum. In this moment of contact, an experience occurs through which the person sutures himself or herself into a larger history ... the person does not simply apprehend a historical narrative but takes on a more personal, deeply felt memory of a past event through which he or she did not live. The resulting prosthetic memory has the ability to shape that person's subjectivity and politics." See Landsberg, *Prosthetic Memory,* 4.

[117] Roger Ebert, "*Defiance,*" *Chicago Sun-Times,* January 14, 2009.

[118] Olaf Hoerschelmann notes that:
"Public memory is an important process through which the collective identity of a community is constructed. Such memories are never univocal or unambiguous, however. Instead, public memory is always contingent and always contested, so that ultimately neither permanent nor stable collective identities exist. Especially through the collective rememberings shown in mass media, public memory can be contested and undermined with countermemories." Hoerschelmann, "*Memoria Dextera Est,*" 78.

[119] Burgoyne's statement in full reads:
"The rising importance and influence of social memory, moreover, has coincided with a widespread cultural desire to reexperience the past in material, sensuous ways, a drive that has been augmented by the mass media and the expanding reach of experiential museums and historical theme parks. With cinema and television increasingly drawn to historical subjects—examples include the advent of the History Channel on cable and the wide-screen success of films such as *Braveheart* and *Schindler's List*—and with the growing popularity of experiential museums and historical reenactments—as exemplified by the Holocaust Museum and the recent D-Day celebrations—the cultural desire to reexperience the past in a sensuous form has become an important, perhaps decisive, factor in the struggle to lay claim to what and how the nation remembers." Robert Burgoyne, *Film Nation:*

Hollywood Looks at U. S. History (Minneapolis: University of Minnesota Press, 1997), 104-105.

[120] Ibid.

[121] Melinda Szaloky, "Sounding Images in Silent Film: Visual Acoustics in Murnau's *Sunrise*," *Cinema Journal* 41:2 (2002): 109-131.

[122] Laura Marks, *The Skin of the* Film (Durham: Duke University Press, 2000), 163-164.

[123] Ibid., 142. In the chapter titled "The Memory of Touch," Marks writes that "cinema itself appeals to contact—to embodied knowledge, and to the sense of touch in particular—in order to reconstruct memories." Ibid., 129.

[124] *Film & History* 32:1 (2002) has a number of articles devoted to the issue of Holocaust memory, including: Joshua Hirsch, "Posttraumatic Cinema and the Holocaust Documentary," *Film & History* 32:1 (2002): 9-20; Frances Guerin, "Reframing the Photographer and His Photographs: *Photographer* (1995)," *Film & History* 32:1 (2002): 43-54; Louisa Rice, "The Voice of Silence: Alain Resnais' *Night and Fog* and Collective Memory in Post-Holocaust France 1944-1974," *Film & History* 32:1 (2002): 22-29; and Lynn Rapaport, "Hollywood's Holocaust: *Schindler's List* and the Construction of Memory." *Film & History* 32:1 (2002): 55-65.

[125] In addition to the scores of texts on the trial, the 42 volume trial transcripts are readily available; see International Military Tribunal, *Trial of the Major War Criminals Before the International Military Tribunal, 14 November 1945—1 October 1946* (Nuremberg: 1947-1949, International Military Tribunal). See also, for example, Telford Taylor's *The Anatomy of the Nuremberg Trials* (New York: Alfred A. Knopf, 1992) for extensive citation of primary sources.

[126] The cast of *Uprising* includes, among others: Hank Azaria (Mordechai Anielewicz); David Schwimmer (Yitzhak Zuckerman); Jon Voight (Major-General Jurgen Stroop); Donald Sutherland (Adam Czerniakow); and Cary Elwes (Dr. Fritz Hippler).

[127] See Steven N. Lipkin, "Defining Docudrama," in Rosenthal, Alan, ed. *Why Docudrama?* (Carbondale: Southern Illinois University Press, 1999), 370-383.

[128] In her assessment of the depiction of the Holocaust in *Schindler's List*, Lynn Rapaport identifies basic questions that arise as repercussions of representation. Rapaport writes: "How does one create a film based on the Holocaust, and make it both morally just and marketable? More generally, what is the role of popular culture in political and social life, and how does it serve the interests of Holocaust education? Is it a legitimate avenue to express a representation of the Holocaust, or do commercial interests and mass appeal trivialize the sacredness of this event?" (55) "These questions arise necessarily because re-creation in Holocaust docudramas such as *Uprising* requires representing what is arguably unrepresentable, and through those depictions, the performance of unimaginably traumatic events. Elie Wiesel argues unequivocally that Holocaust victims must remain a sacred absence, and that their experiences cannot and should not be represented." Rapaport, "Holocaust," 56.

[129] Nichols, *Representing Reality*, 249-250.

[130] See Rapaport, "Holocaust," 56; also Guerin, "Reframing," 48.

[131] See Judith Butler, *Excitable Speech* (New York: Routledge, 1997). Butler notes: "That speech is not the same as writing seems clear, not because the body is present in speech in a way that it is not in writing, but because the oblique relation of the body to speech is itself performed by the utterance, deflected yet carried by the performance itself." (152)

[132] Hirsch, "Posttraumatic Cinema," 11-12.

[133] Ibid., 13.

[134] See, for example, Taylor's approach in *The Anatomy of the Nuremberg Trials.*

[135] In doing so *Nuremberg* echoes what the memoirs of those present at the tribunals also described in focusing on the reactions of defendants to the film; the miniseries becomes more inclusive by including the responses of the prosecutors. Lawrence Douglas notes that the act of witnessing and the credibility of evidence that this action suggests was incorporated into the very structure of the film document: "Lest anyone doubt the veracity of its images, the documentary provides shot after shot of eyewitnesses viewing the very legacy of atrocities that the film records. We watch Generals Eisenhower, Bradley and Patton, examine, ashen-faced, the camps; we track the journey of a delegation of congressmen; we follow the footsteps of GIs filing past rows of bodies." Lawrence Douglas, "Film As Witness: Screening *Nazi Concentration Camps* Before the Nuremberg Tribunal," *The Yale Law Journal* 105 (1995): 471.

[136] See Mark Bowden, *Blackhawk Down: A Story of Modern War*, (New York: New American Library, 1999); and Harold G. Moore, and Joseph L. Galloway, *We Were Soldiers Once ... and Young*, (New York: Random House, 1992).

[137] Gibson's Moore foregrounds the action of leadership, when by comparison, Moore's book focuses on the action that results from his leadership. His self-described role is self-effacing and presented in prose more by implication. See T. Doherty's discussion of both films for a discussion of the Fordian elements that emerge.

[138] The film favors images of charred skin: one GI has to hack away the flesh on his buddy's cheek while it is still flaming from a phosphorous wound; when two others try to move a man who has been accidentally napalmed the flesh on his legs comes off in their hands.

[139] T. Doherty calls them "extraction" films, tracing the need for this narrative arc back to the failed attempt to rescue Iranian hostages in 1980. See Tom Doherty, "The New War Movies as Moral Rearmament: *Black Hawk Down* and *We Were Soldiers, Cineaste* 27:3 (2002): 4-8.

[140] Several critics have suggested that the effort in these films to show the military in a professional light appeals to a post 9/11 audience, as does the implicit argument in both that America needs to be better prepared to counter terrorism. See reviews by Michael Atkinson, "Patriot Shame," *The Village Voice*, March 6-12, 2002; Doherty, "New War Movies," and Michael Massing, "Black Hawk Downer," *The Nation*, February 25, 2002.

[141] Some have suggested that the depiction of combat in these films appears self-limiting; I disagree. For example, Marilyn B. Young writing in *Radical History*

Review states: "Contemporary war movies, from *Saving Private Ryan* to *We Were Soldiers* [...] abstract war from its context, leaving it standing on its own, self-justifying, impervious to doubt, a fact of nature." See Young, "In The Combat Zone," *Radical History Review* 85: 256. Similarly, in describing *Black Hawk*, Dennis Showalter asserts that "we do not need to be informed why the United States is in Mogadishu, because that information is not central to the rangers and the men of Delta Force. Purpose is less important than mission; not why, but what must we do, and how can we get it done?" See Showalter, "Imagery and Realism," *Diplomatic History* 26:4 (Fall 2002): 651.

[142] Moore's book also reiterates the argument of the error of limited aggression, that the war was simply never sufficiently waged.

[143] See, for example, A.O. Scott's review in the *New York Times* of *Soldiers*, "Early in the Vietnam War, On An Ill-Defined Mission," *New York Times*, March 1, 2002.

[144] We have written the only academic books solely on this subject—see Paget, *True Stories,* 1990, and *No Other Way,* 1998; and Lipkin, *Logic,* 2002.

[145] "High Concept" TV drama is resource-heavy in terms of time, money and personnel; "Low Concept" the opposite (see Edgerton, "High Concept," 1991).

[146] Indeed, in November 2007, ninety years after the end of World War One, the BBC could find only five former combatants, all over a hundred years old, to interview in programs leading up to Armistice Day.

[147] Too young himself to be a combatant, but still close to this older generation, Ambrose's admiration for the old soldiers is almost unquestioning. There is no hint of moral disapproval, for example, in the later chapters of the book that detail Easy Company's looting in a defeated Germany. The tone also, we suspect, had something to do with Ambrose growing old himself—he died a year after the launch of the TV series.

[148] Recent European "Historical-Event Television" also owes a debt to oral history. We discuss this phenomenon further later in the article. See also Tobias Ebbrecht, "Docudramatizing History on TV: German and British Docudrama and Historical Event Television in the Memorial Year 2005," *European Journal of Cultural Studies* 10:1 (2007): 35-55; and Tobias Ebbrecht, "History, Public Memory, and Media Event: Codes and Conventions of Historical Event-Television in Germany," *Media History* 13:2/3 (2007): 221-234.

[149] Stephen Ambrose, *Band of Brothers: E Company, 506th Regiment, 101st Airborne From Normandy to Hitler's Eagle's Nest,* (London: Pocket Books, 1992), 310.

[150] Rosenstone, *History On Film/Film On History,* 16.

[151] We are thinking amongst others of the work of historians such as Rosenstone himself, and particularly of Hayden White (see especially White 1973). See Robert Rosenstone, *Revisioning History* (Princeton: Princeton University Press, 1995), and Hayden White, *The Content of the Form* (Baltimore: Johns Hopkins University Press, 1989).

[152] Our emphasis. See BBC website article *"Band of Brothers* Author Dies," dated October 14, 2002: http://news.bbc.co.uk/1/hi/entertainment/arts/2325595.stm - accessed 07/11/2007.

[153] Rupert Smith, "We're In This Together," *Guardian,* May 14, 2001, 16.

[154] We owe the quoted phase to Rory Kelly's presentation at the 'Spielberg at Sixty' conference in Lincoln, November 20, 2007.

[155] Spielberg/Hanks were, of course, no more unique in their field than Ambrose was in his. We would cite Sam Fuller's *The Big Red One* (1980) as a fictional re-working of wartime, documentary, experience. See Marsha Orgeron, "The Most Profound Shock: Traces of the Holocaust in Samuel Fuller's *Verboten! (1955)* and *The Big Red One (1980),"* *Historical Journal of Film, Radio, and Television* 27:4 (2007): 471-511, and Terrence Malik's 1998 *The Thin Red Line* (itself a re-make of a 1964 film—both adaptations of James Jones's experience-soaked 1963 novel) as *avant-garde* flipside to the popular *Ryan* and *Band.*

[156] Ridley Scott's 2001 film *Black Hawk Down* treats this episode.

[157] So, for example, the episode dealing with the airborne Operation Market Garden examines British decision-making leading to disaster at Arnhem; the Bastogne episode faults the lack of preparation on the part of the higher US Army command that led to near-disaster.

[158] See *Logic,* chapter 5 (55-98) for a history of how these values drove the production of American movie-of-the-week docudrama in the 1990s; this, as the next chapter discusses, is also markedly evident in the quick release of *Saving Jessica Lynch.*

[159] The series premiered earlier in the UK (September/October). Transmission in America was delayed owing to the historical event of 9/11.

[160] "Remembrance Sunday" has been on the calendar in Britain since World War 1, taking place on the nearest Sunday to 11 November (this being the day in 1918 when the guns finally stopped firing on the Western Front at 11:00 a.m.). We suggest that "remembrance" is different from "remembering" by virtue of its official dimension as a national event—it is a *public,* not private, exercise of "memory."

[161] The very title "Why We Fight" is an intertextual echo of the wartime documentary film series directed by Hollywood's Frank Capra.

[162] Marsha Orgeron gives an account of Samuel Fuller's wrestling with his felt responsibility as a witness of wartime atrocity in his films *Verboten!* (1955) and *The Big Red One* (1980). In the latter, Fuller stages a very similar moment of discovery to that in *Band* (Orgeron, "Shock," 484-486).

[163] Rosenstone, *History on Film/Film on History,* 106.

[164] Ibid., 107.

[165] Smith, "We're in This," 16.

[166] Ebbrecht, "Docudramatizing History" and "History, Public Memory."

[167] Jon Dovey, *Freakshow: First Person Media and Factual Television* (London: Pluto Press, 2000).

[168] James Rampton, "Shooting War," *Radio Times,* September 29-October 5, 2001, 15—our emphasis.

[169] John Corner, "Backward Looks: Mediating the Past," *Media Culture and Society* 28:3 (2006): 467—our emphasis.
[170] Email to Derek Paget, 15 November 2007.
[171] Ebbrecht "History, Public Memory," 223—our emphasis).
[172] This is borne out in other television cultures— Witness/Survivor speaking direct to camera has been a feature of, for example, a series of British-made "Historical-Event" docudramas: in *Dunkirk* (2004), *D-Day— 6/6/44* (2004) and *Hiroshima* (2005), to name but three BBC films, the tropes described and analyzed by Ebbrecht—witness testimony amongst them—are also to be found.
[173] Ebbrecht, "Docudramatizing History," 35.
[174] Ebbrecht, "History, Public Memory," 223.
[175] Ibid., 221.
[176] Ibid., 224.
[177] Ebbrecht, "Docudramatizing History," 37.
[178] Ibid.
[179] Richard Holmes, Letter, *Radio Times*, January 5-11, 2002, 7.
[180] Rick Bragg, *I Am A Soldier, Too: The Jessica Lynch Story* (New York: Knopf, 2003).
[181] See, for example, http://www.jessica-lynch.com/; http://www.disinfopedia.org/wiki.phtml?title=Jessica_Lynch; http://www.jessica-lynch.com/photos.html; http://jessicalynch.newstrove.com/; etc.
[182] "Seven Theses About Border Genres / Five Modest Proposals About Docudrama," *Screening the Past*, Issue 14, 2002, http://www.latrobe.edu.au/screeningthepast/firstrelease/fr0902/paget/dpfr14b.htm.
[183] See Lipkin, *Logic*, Chapt. 5, "Rootable, Relatable, Promotable Docudrama: The MOW Mantra As Rhetorical Practice," 55-98.
[184] "Rescued POW Flown to Germany," BBC News, *World Edition*, April 3, 2003, http://news.bbc.co.uk/2hi/middle_east/2908477.stm
[185] "Rescued POW Has First Surgery," CNN.com, April 3, 2003, http://www.cnn.com/2003/US/South/04/03/sprj.irq.rescue
[186] "The Truth About Jessica," *The Guardian Unlimited*, May 15, 2003.
[187] Ibid.; see as well as Robert Scheer, "Saving Private Lynch, Take 2," http://www.alternet.org/story/15958.
[188] See Lipkin, *Logic,* 150 (note 4).
[189] Ibid., 149.
[190] Ibid., 13; 23-27. Docudramas also will sequence the real and what it must re-create, that is, alternate between re-created and actual footage, so that the modeled material benefits from its literal closeness to documentary imagery. The interviews with Easy Company veterans that open each episode of *Band of Brothers* set up this strategy. For better or worse, Oliver Stone used sequencing throughout *JFK* as a means to augment the authenticity of the claims the film would forward. Another warranting strategy, interaction, places actual and re-created elements within the mise en scene, so that real-life principals move through scenes with actors (the real Jim Garrison in *JFK*), or actors move through the actual locations where the re-created events originally occurred (the Illinois State

Penitentiary in *Call Northside 777*; the town hall with its memorial wall in *Perfect Storm*).

[191] While the controversies surrounding works such as *JFK* (O. Stone, 1991), *Mississippi Burning* (A. Parker, 1988), and *The People vs. Larry Flynt* (M. Forman, 1996) have been notorious because critics have questioned the closeness of their re-creations to the known actuality they reference, there have also been concerns raised on the same basis about *The Insider* (M. Mann, 1999), *The Hurricane* (N. Jewison, 1999), and *A Beautiful Mind* (R. Howard, 2001). On *The Insider*, see http://www.suntimes.com/ebert/ebert_reviews/1999/11/110506.html; on *A Beautiful Mind*, see *The New York Times,* December 21, 2002: "From Math to Madness, and Back;" on *The Hurricane*, see http://www.suntimes.com/ebert/ebert_reviews/2000/01/010705.html.

[192] Other war-related works of note aired in the three-year period after May 2000 include: *Submerged*; *Haven*; *Nuremberg*; *Uprising*; *Gathering Storm*; *One Night in Baghdad*; *Daughter from Da Nang*; *Out of the Ashes*; and *Band of Brothers*.

[193] The American public viewed the impact of its military in Bosnia during the Clinton administration as it confronted the holocaust-like ethnic cleansing there and the consequent need for war crimes tribunals. Involvement in Mogadishu, Somalia in 1993 publicized the impotence of the American army through widely-seen images of the corpse of an American GI being dragged through the streets.

[194] In the first half of 2004 news coverage of the war in Iraq continued to attempt to grapple with the interrelationship of victims, images of American women in the military, and the repercussions of questionable leadership. Incidents of prisoner abuse at Abu Ghraib brought to the world's attention the countless replays of photographs of Private Lyndie England "handling" Iraqi prisoners, leading to her court martial. England's (and others') defense, that they were following the dictates of army command structure, immediately brought attention to (and the replacement of) General Janis Karpinski, who had been in charge of the prison when the abuses occurred. Stories (and photographs) of Lynch as her hearings progressed in August, 2004 consistently refer to her advanced pregnancy, positioning England as both perpetrator and victim in this chapter of the war.

[195] See "Jessica Lynch Tells Her Story," *Today/MSNBC News*, November 12, 2003, http://msnbc.msn.com/id/3475980/ for a transcript of her interview with Katie Couric.

[196] Interview with the author, October 14, 2009.

[197] Interview with the author, March 24, 2010.

[198] George Custen, *Bio/Pic; How Hollywood Constructed Public History* (New Brunswick: Rutgers University Press, 1992), 8.

[199] See, for example, C. Taylor, *"Ray,"* *salon.com*, October 29, 2004, http://dir.sa.on.com/story/ent/moview/review/2004/10/29/ray/index.html; Mick LaSalle, "Jamie Foxx Plays It Just Right," *San Francisco Chronicle*, October 29, 2004, http://www.sfgate.com/cgi-bin/article.cgi?f=/c/a/2004/11/19/ddg659t89cl.dtl;   M. Dujsik, *"Beyond the Sea,"* http://mart-reviews-movies.tripod.com/reviews/b/beyondsea.htm.

[200] Custen, *Bio/Pic,* 148-149.

[201] Ibid., 17.

[202] Ibid., 153.

[203] Ibid., 148-149.

[204] Ibid., 17.

[205] For example, in a review of Thomas Doherty's *Cold War, Cool Medium: Television, McCarthyism, and American Culture* (New York: Columbia University Press, 2003), Christine Becker writes: "Murrow's legendary *"See It Now"* takedown of McCarthy packaged together McCarthy's own venomous and contradictory words, and the episode capped off by a stirring, poetic speech by Murrow." From *Film Quarterly* 59:1 (2005): 55-56.

[206] See Doherty on the film's chronology of these events.

[207] See Joseph E. Persico, *Edward R. Murrow: An American Original* (New York: McGraw-Hill, 1988), 157, and A. M. Sperber, *Murrow: His Life and Times* (New York: Freundlich Books, 1986), 356. Sperber writes here: "The mike fright that beset him in radio intensified before the camera."

[208] Sperber, *Murrow,* 76 and 158-170; Persico, *Murrow,* 192.

[209] Sperber, *Murrow,* 229-30; Persico, *Murrow,* 218; 240.

[210] Murrow worked for the Emergency Committee in Aid of Displaced German Scholars. See Sperber, pp. 51-58.

[211] The desire for a 50s film "look" led to a search for the lenses Godard had used in 50s films. See David Carr, "A Ringside Seat For Murrow vs. McCarthy," *New York Times,* September 14, 2005, Arts 12; 26.

[212] For a discussion of sequencing warrants see Lipkin, *Logic,* 24-25.

INDEX